# Education for Capability

# Education for Capability

Edited for
The RSA (The Royal Society for the
encouragement of Arts,
Manufactures and Commerce)

by
Tyrrell Burgess

**NFER–NELSON**

Published by The NFER–NELSON Publishing Company Ltd.,
Darville House, 2 Oxford Road East,
Windsor, Berkshire SL4 1DF, England.

and in the United States of America by

NFER-NELSON, 242 Cherry Street, Philadelphia, PA 19106–1906.
Tel: (215) 238 0939. Telex: 244489.

First Published 1986
© 1986 Royal Society of Arts

Library of Congress Cataloging in Publication Data

Main entry under title:

Education for capability.

   1. Education – Great Britain – Aims and objectives.
2. Competency based education – Great Britain.
3. Labor supply – Great Britain – Effect of education on.
I. Burgess, Tyrrell. II. Royal Society of Arts (Great Britain)
LA632.E373   1986        370'.941        85–215588
ISBN 0–7005–0688–8

Photoset by David John Services Ltd., Maidenhead, Berks, UK.

Printed in Great Britain by A. Wheaton & Co. Ltd., Exeter

ISBN 0 7005 0688 8
Code 8190 02 1

# Foreword

A society whose aims are the 'encouragement of Arts, Manufactures and Commerce' has a natural interest in what people *do* as well as what they *know*. From its recognition of practical achievement in the eighteenth century, through its advocacy of technical education and training in the last century, to much of the work of its Examinations Board today, the RSA has valued and encouraged competence.

I think, therefore, that the Society has been a most appropriate base from which to launch the *Education for Capability* campaign. Now, after five years of effort, it is excellent that our Education for Capability Committee should collect together in this volume an account of its thinking, principles and experience.

The book as a whole has been inspired and shaped by the Committee and, in particular, by one of its members, Tyrrell Burgess, who has acted as editor. The contributions represent the views of the individuals concerned.

It is the aims and purpose of *Education for Capability*, as defined on page *ix*, which the Society supports and promotes. Education for Capability is a challenge to the education system. This book will give that challenge greater impetus.

*Sir Peter Baldwin KCB, Chairman of Council*

*1985*

# Contents

# Education for Capability Manifesto

*There is a serious imbalance in Britain today in the full process which is described by the two words 'education' and 'training'. The idea of the 'educated person' is that of a scholarly individual who has been neither educated nor trained to exercise useful skills; who is able to understand but not to act. Young people in secondary or higher education increasingly specialize, and do so too often in ways which mean that they are taught to practise only the skills of scholarship and science. They acquire knowledge of particular subjects, but are not equipped to use knowledge in ways which are relevant to the world outside the education system.*

*This imbalance is harmful to individuals, to industry and to society. A well-balanced education should, of course, embrace analysis and the acquisition of knowledge. But it must also include the exercise of creative skills, the competence to undertake and complete tasks and the ability to cope with everyday life; and also doing all these things in co-operation with others.*

*There exists in its own right a culture which is concerned with doing, making and organizing and the creative arts. This culture emphasizes the day-to-day management of affairs, the formulation and solution of problems and the design, manufacture and marketing of goods and services.*

*Educators should spend more time preparing people in this way for a life outside the education system. The country would benefit significantly in economic terms from what is here described as Education for Capability.*

# Introduction

*Tyrrell Burgess*

Our object in this book is to restore hope to education. It is needed, because at present education is under fire from all sides. This is not altogether a novel situation: the first chapters of this book show how longstanding the criticism is. What is new is the energy with which the criticisms are being pursued and the failure of any new initiatives, some of them very costly, to generate commensurate enthusiasm or support.

The restoration of hope depends upon two things: a real understanding of the causes of the present discontents, and persuasive proposals for remedying them.

Certainly the history of education has been one of hope and disillusion. The hope is that it can offer improvement to both individuals and society: it is sought as a remedy for personal and social ills. In times of hope central and local government increases educational spending. Electoral promises can be summed up in one word: more. Public inquiries on the salaries of teachers recommend large increases. In times of disillusion people begin to wonder whether education does not cost too much, or whether we are getting value for money. There are complaints that education is offering no solution to serious problems, like unemployment or urban crime. Individuals begin to doubt whether the rewards of education are worth the tedium of pursuing it.

The authors of this book believe that there is a serious imbalance in British education and training, which is itself responsible for the destruction of hope and the deepening of disillusion. The idea of the 'educated man' has been that of a scholarly, leisured individual who has not been educated to exercise useful skills. Those who study in secondary schools or higher education increasingly specialize, so that they can then practise only the skills of scholarship; they are trained to research rather than to act. Their knowledge of a particular area of study does not include ways of thinking and working which are apt outside the education system itself. Education has tended to concentrate on analysis, criticism and the acquisition of knowledge, and to neglect the formulation and solution of problems: doing, making and organizing; and constructive and creative activity in general. This inhibits the satisfaction derived from personal capability and denies to society the benefits of competence. It is thus damaging to individuals and to society.

These beliefs about education led, some years ago, to the formation of the 'Education for Capability' movement, now established under the auspices of the Royal Society of Arts. The movement was launched with the publication of a widely supported manifesto (see pp.*ix* and 177) and has continued since through a scheme of recognition of good practice, through newsletters and conferences and in many other ways, including this book. We believe that our sense of the imbalance in education is widely shared.

Evidence of this comes from pupils, students and their parents, from teachers and employers, and it is possible here to indicate only the range and nature of their criticisms. Let us start with pupils at school. There has been a number of serious studies of what pupils think and want, from the Schools Council inquiry seventeen years ago[1] to John Raven's research published in 1977[2]. These reveal that pupils have clear and coherent views about what school is for and that they feel that the schools themselves have other objects. In particular, pupils wanted an education which enabled them to deal with their personal problems, to have and hold a job, to apply their knowledge, and to be the confident masters rather than the slaves of circumstance. Generally speaking, parents agreed with their children in this. There have been similar surveys[3] of the attitudes of older students. They, too, demand 'relevance'. They complain that their courses tend towards the mere accumulation of knowledge, are overcrowded with detail and give little time to think. Many see their educational experience as 'tricks and dodges' and their courses as consisting of anything that could attract a twenty-minute question in the final examination. They may find that having knowledge does not at all enable them to apply it: even when theory and practice are integrated, students may not be able either to apply the theory or to describe and defend their practice. Many come to fear that their courses are directed to no vocational end, and even those on a supposedly vocational course may see its relevance as spurious because they seem to get no nearer to the practice of their specialism. Other students complain of narrowness and stultification. They complain that final examinations frequently demand little more than memory, and they hanker for more command over their educational experience.

Many of these criticisms are echoed by teachers. Those in secondary schools, in particular, see themselves as victims of external circumstance. They complain of the tyranny of society which requires them to be not so much educators as selectors, serving the division of labour, and of an examination system which is the expression of this tyranny. As John Raven found, teachers are conscious that they do not concentrate on the objectives they consider to be most important, and he rightly says that the consequences of this are insidiously demoralizing.

It is often claimed that the perversion of education by selection is supported by employers, who express their demands in terms of certificates, diplomas and degrees. This is true, but it conceals the criticism which employers have of the system which offers these certificates.[4] What employers typically say is that they take the possession of a certificate or a degree as a very general indication of a level of capacity and application. They do not see it as indicating the acquisition of any information or skill that can be productively used. Employers assert that it is they who have to educate and train the young person who comes to them, whether he has CSE or a degree. Many go further, and claim that the more education a young person has received the less fitted he is for the problems that he has to face as an employee. On this view an employer takes a graduate rather than a non-graduate only because he imagines that the qualification is an indication of capacity: he fears that much will have to be done to eliminate the incompetence systematically induced by the process of graduation.

To these specific criticisms are added more general ones. There are those who regard education as having developed to the point of being an expensive luxury. There are others who seek a solution in accepting it as a selective process and wish to concentrate on

4 Education for Capability

making the selection more 'efficient'. There are many, on all sides, who are concerned about the quality of education and ways in which this can be measured. Many reformers are bewildered by the realization that the expansion of education has not itself led to a more rational, egalitarian or viable society. At the extremes there are those who believe that education can be saved only by removing it altogether form its institutional framework: they would de-school education and society.

More recently there has been systematic pressure for change, at all levels of education, from central government. Its consistent concerns have related to the character, quality and relevance of education and to its cost. Unhappily, many of its initiatives – in reforming examinations, in vocational education and elsewhere – are already generating the familiar disillusionment.

This book seeks, first, to establish the lessons of the past and the challenge of the future; and, second, to offer ways in which improvement might be sought. In other words, it faces disenchantment and seeks to create hope. The third task of the book is to describe some solutions in practice, drawn from the experience of the RSA Education for Capability Recognition Scheme. Whatever the general state of education, there are, buried away in the system at all stages, often unknown and unacknowledged, the projects and programmes which offer hope for the future. Throughout the system, people have found it possible to use to good advantage the circumstances in which they find themselves. Our Recognition Scheme rests on the belief that it is from the energy, imagination and ability of individuals that desirable change must come.

This is not yet a general view. At present remedies are sought elsewhere. One is the accelerating increase in centralized direction and control of what is taught and how it is assessed. Elements of this approach include recommendations for a 'core' curriculum, the reform of external examinations at sixteen-plus and the use of the Manpower Services Commission to direct vocational education. Another favourite remedy is sought in greater expenditure. This approach is more popular outside than inside government, but despite economies expenditure per pupil or student is in fact increasing. The argument for greater spending is that any improvement in the output of education must depend upon increasing the inputs. It is even held that in changing social

circumstances, more expense is needed to prevent deterioration.
A third remedy is to increase the 'quality' of teachers by better
initial training, by multiplying in-service courses and by
conducting 'performance reviews' of schools and assessments of
individual teachers.

All these remedies are applied 'from the top down'. They
assume that the Secretary of State, or a local education authority,
knows or can discover what schools should offer and how; that a
national or local decision to spend more will naturally produce a
better education; that the key to greater learning lies in better
teachers, so that teachers must be trained, retrained, assessed and
reviewed. They have been pursued for some years with vigour:
centralization has increased, spending on education and training
has risen while numbers fall, and teachers are trained – and nagged
– into doing better. Indeed, there is now enough experience to
suggest that by themselves they are not enough.

There have been many reforms of the public system of external
examinations now represented by GCE 'O' level and CSE: no-one
has ever been able to show that standards have risen as a
consequence. The examinations themselves are discredited in
government, in the schools and among pupils – especially among
'successful' pupils. The reformed system now promised will
involve an elaborate hunt for the 'criterion-referencing' of
standards, but without any hope that standards will, in fact, be
raised. An acceptable 'core' curriculum must be so general as to
conceal the real problems. The 'vocational' offerings of the MSC
are beginning to generate a disillusionment among the young
comparable with that surrounding academic exam. syllabuses.

If money could have done the trick, it would have done it by
now. The education service is opulent as never before. Huge
increases are needed to produce trivial improvement. There is no
imaginable level of expenditure that would make improvement
inevitable.

There can be many arguments about the quality of in-service
training. The trouble is that such training bumps up against the
logical and practical difficulty that efforts to improve teachers do
not directly or necessarily improve the performance of students. If
the latter is what is required, why not do it directly?

The experience of the Education for Capability movement
suggests that these 'top down' remedies, for all the effort and

resources that go into them, are not enough. Lasting reform must come from the bottom up; that is, from individuals and groups making the best of their own circumstances. Indeed, the problem is to see that the traditional approaches do not stifle individual and local initiative.

I would, myself, go further than this and say that education will improve only if learners are able to take more responsibility for their own learning. This means giving substance to those parts of the Education Acts which are concerned with the suitability of education to the age, ability and aptitude of individual students and with the wishes of their parents. Fortunately, this remedy, too, is being pursued through official policy, this time on records of achievement. It may be that individual teachers and schools will be able to use the new policy to develop the individual capabilities of their pupils and students.

I am convinced that the greatest resource in education is not the 'system', or money, or even teachers: it is the students. It is only if their characters, capacities, knowledge, energies and hopes can be harnessed that education can take place at all. Their desire to learn, so notably absent at present, can be enhanced if they themselves take responsibility for their own learning. What this means is that teachers must get used to listening to what students are saying.

A convenient moment for this, though not the only one, is the 'options' stage at the end of the third year at secondary school. At present, students have then to make a debilitating choice between more or less attractive packages. It could and should be a time in which young people reflect, with their parents and teachers, on what it is they bring to the last two years of their compulsory schooling, what it is they wish to be and to do at the end of it, and what would enable them to get from one to the other.

An educational programme is best thought of as a solution to some problem or problems, and the problems that most people care about are the ones that face them directly. It is hard to see to what problems 'O' level history is a solution.

Fortunately there is a recent initiative by the Secretary of State which can be turned to advantage. The importance of the new policy on records of achievement is that it could transform students' views of themselves and the purposes of their education. Even as it stands, it offers some hope of recognizing the nine-tenths or more of the whole person which is neglected by examination courses and unassessed by the examinations themselves. But its promise will be unrealized if the record remains the passive filling-up of a form or becomes the accumulation of report-like judgements from teachers. Instead, the recording can and should be the summarized evidence of achievement in a course which students have planned and for which they are responsible.

By contrast, every step towards centralized control or guidance, every increase in the 'training' of serving teachers, threatens this outcome. Every assertion that improvement depends upon increased expenditure dooms another generation to frustration and apathy. The challenge to education is to find ways of releasing and enhancing the capabilities of young people. It is the object of this book to hint at what might happen if this were generally achieved.

**References**

1  SCHOOLS COUNCIL (1968). *Young School Leavers: Report of an Enquiry carried out for the Schools Council by the Government Social Survey*. Enquiry 1, HMSO.
2  RAVEN, J. (1977).*Education Values and Society: The Objectives of Education and the Nature and Development of Competence*. London: H K Lewis.
3  BEARD, R. (1970). *Teaching and Learning in Higher Education*. Harmondsworth: Penguin.
4  This was the almost unanimous view, for example, of those employers whom my colleagues and I consulted on our proposal to create a new course leading to a Diploma of Higher Education.

# PART ONE:   The Problem

## The Burden of the Past

## The Challenge of Change

# CHAPTER 1
# The Organizational Failure
*Correlli Barnett*

A capable person is one who can tackle both the practical situations of life and the operational problems of a particular professional sphere. A country like Great Britain requires individual and collective capability at the business of being an advanced industrial economy, and in the process of designing, making and marketing products and services that people will wish to buy in preference to rival ones.

The question is whether Britain is capable as an advanced industrial nation, or not. Britain has now sunk to fourteenth place in the non-Communist world in terms of GNP per head. Our manufacturing output is now barely a third of West Germany's, although our national population is little smaller. The evidence of our incapability fills our newspapers and journals week after week. In one industry after another, where comparison is possible, British productivity is seen to be lower than that of other countries. Reports speak of inefficiency as deeply embedded in our national life-style.

Inferiority is not due to lack of investment. Bacon and Eltis found that while machine tools in British factories were newer than in America, output in the United States was three times higher. They found no evidence that the average age and service life of manufacturing capital stock in the two countries can explain the productivity differences. An MTRA Report in 1966 showed that machine tools in the United Kingdom are utilized for only 40 per cent of the time available.[1] While some industries may have gone short of investment, the evidence appears to show that we fail to wring maximum production out of the plant we have; in other words, our problem really is incapability.

Nor can it be argued that European rivals lost all their old plant in the war and re-equipped from scratch with Marshall Aid. Only 15–20 per cent of Germany's industrial equipment was damaged beyond repair in the war, while West Germany received only some two-thirds the amount of Marshall aid that Great Britain did: 1.7 billion dollars as against 2.7 billion. In the five years after the Second World War Britain received in loans and grants from all sources some 8 billion dollars. That we could receive so much and yet end up so unsuccessful must be a further pointer that our real problem is indeed a pervasive incapability.

At a time of high unemployment there is a persistent shortage of skilled workers. At every level of British industry there is either a shortage of skilled and appropriately qualified personnel or, even if they have the paper technical qualifications, they tend in fact to be of lower personal calibre and of lower status within the firm than their European opposite numbers.

This reflects on our education in two ways. In the first place our education fails to provide the right quantities, and the right balance, of the appropriately skilled personnel we need for industrial capability. Secondly, the general ethos and thrust of British education are, if anything, hostile to industry and careers in industry. As a result, too small a proportion of the national talent seeks a life in manufacture. The percentage of professional engineers employed in production actually fell from 9 per cent in 1966 to 6 per cent in 1975. The proportion of all graduates entering manufacturing fell from about 40 per cent in the years up to 1970 to only 26 per cent in 1973.[2] There are signs that very recently attitudes towards careers in industry may be changing, but it is too soon to say how permanent this will prove.

At present, therefore, we are *not* educating for capability, and we are paying the price for it in chronic industrial unsuccess.

The main purpose of this chapter is to show that there is nothing novel about this. Our comparative lack of capability as an industrial society is not a matter of the post-war era, but dates back before 1850, to the very moment when we lost our early technological monopoly and began to face rivals. And right from that time, too, the quality, quantity and values of British education have been a key factor in that lack of capability.

In the initial phase of industrialization between 1760 and 1840 formal education and training were not of decisive importance because, of its nature, a primitive stage of machine-building and manufacturing operation required little more than the *native* capability of resourceful practical men; craftsmen turning old skills to new purposes; self-educated rule-of-thumb. Our entrepreneurs built their businesses by similar commercial methods, starting small as a local tradesman or craftsman, and expanding by grace of native 'nous'. It is true that some early industrial figures were interested in the scientific developments of the time. Yet science itself in the late eighteenth century was, like industry, a matter of self-education and private experiment: a superior form of rule-of-thumb.

It therefore hardly mattered that in this period there was little basic education for the masses; that grammar schools and public schools were mostly in decay and anyway taught an irrelevant syllabus of Greek and Latin; and that Oxbridge lay in gouty slumber.

There arose in British industry right from the start, therefore, a tradition of the resourceful amateur, the man who learned on the job and passed on his knowledge verbally to the next generation as a craft 'mystery' in the medieval style, rather than the man specially and systematically trained for the rôle, so that practical application was backed by theoretical understanding. This was true all the way from boardroom to workbench. From this derived a potent British myth: that of 'the practical man'. But this meant 'practicality'. The cult of the practical man carried with it, contrariwise, a positive mistrust of the application of intellectual study and scientific research to industrial operations; a deep suspicion of the very kind of highly trained and professionally educated man European and American industry looked for from the start. In 1850 the *Economist* was writing that 'the education which fits men to perform their duties in life is not to be got in school, but in the counting-houses and lawyer's office, in the shop or the factory'.

But in the course of the first half of the nineteenth century industrial products and processes were passing beyond the primitive stage of bolting on more plates when the boiler burst, or taking something out of the furnace when old Joe reckoned the colour was right. What was now needed was systematic formal training in basic scientific and engineering principles and in specialized applications like metallurgy, the chemical industry, machine design and manufacture, production methods, and a need for intimate links between experimental science, technical education and the world of industry. As early as 1835 we find Richard Cobden warning, after a visit to America, that 'our only chance of national prosperity lies in the timely remodelling of our system, so as to put it as nearly as possible upon an equality with the improved management of the Americans'.[3] Just two years after the Great Exhibition of 1851 had seemed to consummate the triumph of British technology, Dr Lyon Playfair wrote in his book *Industrial Education on the Continent* that European industry was bound to overtake Britain if she failed to alter her outlook and methods.[4] Thus perceptive critics in Britain saw as early as this the connection between education for capability and industrial success.

Unfortunately, it was not just critics but the State and public opinion in general that had seen the connection abroad, and throughout the early nineteenth century European countries and America were creating institutions for technical education that would turn out '*educated* practical men'; institutions, moreover, for technical education at the highest level. The French *Ecole Polytechnique*, with its still continuing enormous influence and prestige, was founded in 1794; the Polytechnische Institut of Vienna in 1815; and the Technische Hochschule at Karlsruhe in 1825, at Dresden in 1828, Stuttgart in 1829. All the German technical high schools were advancing towards university rank, though it would be 1890 before they acquired the right to grant degrees. In 1855 the Zürich Polytechnikum was founded; the prototype for all the polytechnics that were to proliferate in Europe, expecially in Germany. And although American society was so different from German, it was from the German model that America adapted her own education institutions in the nineteenth century. We may note that MIT was founded in 1865.

However, it was not simply technical education which our rivals were providing for their peoples, but complete and coherent national systems of education. By 1850 most European countries had followed the Prussian example of universal state primary education as the base of the educational pyramid, and widespread state secondary schools as the necessary foundation for technical and higher education.

In Britain, by contrast, no such educational advance had taken place by the 1850s. Primary education was still left to the churches, and in 1851 only about half the children between the ages of three and thirteen in England and Wales were getting any kind of education at all. Secondary education (outside the 'public' schools) consisted of a random patchwork of ancient grammar schools, many in decay, and private schools. With regard to technical education there were merely local mechanics' institutes and scientific societies, the Royal School of Mines and examining bodies like the Royal Society of Arts. The new University of Durham had been founded to supply clergymen.

Yet there *had* been an educational revolution in Britain since the 1820s: the reform and expansion of the public schools which produced the British governing élite. And it is in the nature of the Victorian public school that we find the other key factor explaining why Britain was so slow and so inadequate in educating for industrial capability. The Victorian public school was inspired by the religious and moral idealism of the Romantic Movement. It turned away from the realities of the industrialized world of the era and from such topics as science and technology. It did not set out to equip their pupils to lead great industrial enterprises or a great industrial nation, but to turn them into Christian gentlemen able to govern the Empire and ornament the ancient professions like the Church and the Law. One must also take note here of the influence of liberal *laissez-faire* doctrine, with its condemnation of state intervention in such matters as education, which served to supplement industry's own complete lack of demand for technical education.

What were the effects, by the 1860s, of this virtual absence in Britain of all kinds of education for capability? Royal Commissions of the time tell us with vast thoroughness and a mass of evidence. The Schools Inquiry Commission of 1868 said this:

'We are bound to add that our evidence appears to show that our industrial classes have not even the basis of sound general education on which alone technical education can rest . . . In fact our deficiency is not merely a deficiency in technical education, but . . . in general intelligence, and unless we remedy this want we shall gradually but surely find that our undeniable superiority in wealth and perhaps in energy will not save us from decline.'5

Pretty prophetic, one might think! By way of contrast, the Royal Commission on Technical Education of 1884 wrote thus of Germany:

'The one point in which Germany is overwhelmingly superior to England is in schools, and in the education of all classes of the people. The dense ignorance so common among workmen in England is unknown . . .'[6]

So much then for the rank and file of British industry a hundred years ago. Of what we should call 'middle management', the House of Commons Select Committee on Scientific Instruction of 1867–8 observed:

'Unfortunately this division may be disposed of in a very few words . . . Its members have either risen from the rank of foreman or workman, or they are an off-shoot from the class of smaller tradesmen, clerks, etc . . .'[7]

And of top managers the same committee said that if they had risen from the ranks:

'. . . any knowledge of scientific principles which they may have acquired is generally the result of solitary reading, and of observation of the facts with which their pursuits have made them familiar.'[8]

However,

'more generally, the training of the capitalists and of the managers of their class had been that of the higher secondary schools . . .'[9]

The cumulative evidence that we were already being surpassed technologically and that our want of education had much to do with this did have its effect between 1870 and the outbreak of the Great War. Reform did take place; new institutions *were* created. However, the improvements never came soon enough, nor on a large enough scale, nor on a sufficiently comprehensive plan. One may broadly say that in every field of education we continued to be some fifty years or more behind our rivals. Let me briefly summarize. Take primary education, the basis of everything: the 1870 Education Act did *not* set up universal state primary education as Prussia had at the beginning of the century, but only provided funds out of the rates to set up new schools to supplement existing church schools. It was not until 1880 that there were enough school places for primary education to be made compulsory. By 1900 the 'Board Schools' were educating almost as many children as the church schools, and had become free. However, these schools offered education at rock-bottom standards, drilling dirty and nit-ridden children through the three R's. Compare a Royal Commission's comment on a Swiss primary school several years earlier: 'We were particularly struck by the clean and tidy appearance of the boys and there was difficulty in realizing that the school consisted mainly of children of the lower classes.'[10] In 1894 the odds against an English elementary school child getting a scholarship to a secondary school were 270 to one against.

This was because despite reforms of the old grammar school and other piecemeal improvements, it was not until the 1902 Education Act that Britain finally began to set up a coherent system of state secondary education. Even this reform fell short of expectations, because in 1913 transfers from elementary schools to secondary were only a quarter of the total hoped for. In 1909 three-quarters of English young people between fourteen and seventeen were under no kind of education at all.

So the base of the educational pyramid continued to be much too narrow. Reforms in technical and university education were no less piecemeal and inadequate. All the Royal Commission trumpetings in the 1880s resulted in the Technical Instruction Act by which local authorities were left to expand technical education on a penny rate and, after 1890, on the proceeds from the duty on whisky. Instead of a complete and coherent system of technical education on the German model, all we had by 1902, according to one authority, amounted 'with a few brilliant exceptions such as Owen's College, Manchester, to little more than a congeries of technical and literary classes; a small number of polytechnics mainly in London; a rather large number of organized science schools and evening science and art classes . . . .'[11]

And despite the 1902 Education Act, fewer than twenty

first-class technical schools were built in Britain between 1902 and 1918. The Imperial College of Science and Technology was founded only in 1903. In 1908, when Germany possessed ten technical high schools of university rank, with some 14,000 students, Britain still had no such institutions, but instead thirty-one re-organized technical schools with a total of 2,768 students.

Development of traditional universities by no means made up the difference. Oxford and Cambridge, like the public schools, were very late and reluctant to introduce science and modern studies like languages, let alone what the Germans call 'Technik'. The first physics classes in the Clarendon Laboratory took place in 1870; next year the building of the Cavendish at Cambridge was begun. In the traditionally highly academic environment of Oxbridge, it was not so much 'Technik' – the industrial and operational aspects of science – that prospered as pure research. Another mandarinism thus took its place alongside the classics and mathematics; another form of intellectual snobbery to entice the gifted away from careers in manufacturing industry. In 1903 a private conference was held in Cambridge on the gulf between Cambridge and industry. The Professor of Chemistry said at this meeting that he agreed 'with all the Vice-Chancellor had said as to the complaint of men engaged in business of various kinds that the University does not provide an education for their sons suited to their needs . . .'[12]

The years from 1870 to 1900 saw the piecemeal founding of the first wave of 'red-brick' universities or university colleges: Birmingham, Aberystwyth, Cardiff and Bangor. In 1897 the British government expended £26,000 in grants to universities; the Germans nearly half a million. In 1902 Germany possessed twenty-two universities for a population of some fifty million; England seven for a population of thirty-one million. The second wave of red-brick universities only followed the 1902 Education Act.

Britain therefore entered the twentieth century an ill-educated, one might say ignorant, nation compared with its rivals; and particularly weak in those key areas of education on which industrial success depends. We see in these failures the combined baneful effects of liberal *laissez-faire*'s reluctance to embark on large-scale state education at all levels, the 'practical man's' scorn for technical education, and a public-school-educated governing élite's lack of comprehension that Britain stood or fell by her industrial capability. And what by 1914 had been the cumulative penalty for our failure to educate for capability? A progressive defeat in the advanced technological markets of the world such as Europe and America and a retreat to the less demanding markets of backward regions; and – something which strikes a familiar note today – a progressive invasion of the British home market by foreign technology. When we embarked on industrial mobilization for munitions production during the Great War the extent of our own deficiencies and our dependence on foreign sources for advanced technology became painfully manifest to the Government. Britain produced only half the German quantity of steel and even then neither of the quality nor the specialized kinds produced in Germany. According to the official *History of the Ministry of Munitions*:

'British manufacturers were behind other countries in research, plant and method. Many of the iron and steel firms were working on a small scale, old systems and uneconomical plant, their cost of production being so high that competition with the steel works of the United States and Germany was becoming impossible.'[13]

The Iron and Steel Industrial Committee in 1917 found many iron-masters ignorant of the basic scientific principles underlying their own operations. It is a sombre fact that Britain only averted defeat in the Great War before 1916 by importing American steel and shells.

Lack of mass-production light-engineering factories that could be switched to shell-machining and fuse making, like the German clock and toy industries, forced Britain to create wartime factories for the purpose. This attempt immediately uncovered another deficiency: there was no modern machine-tool industry capable of supplying the advanced machinery. As the *History of the Ministry of Munitions* put it, 'The British machine-tool market was conservative both as regards novelty in design and quantity of output.'[14] Before the war, advanced machine-tools had been imported from Germany and the United States. Since machine-tools are the key to many kinds of large-scale provision manufacture, it was only because of purchases of American, Swiss and Swedish machine-tools that the wartime munitions effort did not break down. But shortages continued to have a throttling effect in many fields.

Except for one factory, Britain had come to depend entirely on Germany for ball-bearings – an absolute essential of modern technology. In 1914 she was forced to turn to Swiss and Swedish sources until she could expand her own industry. As late as 1917 Swedish supplies were more than half those of home production, and in the last year of the war shortages of ball-bearings were another throttle on the production of internal combustion engines, tanks and aircraft. Yet another virtually total British lack in 1914 was a magneto industry. There was but one British firm with an annual production of just over a thousand of a simple type. Again Britain had come to depend on Germany. In any case, British resources in internal combustion manufacture were themselves small, as was the aircraft industry. Until 1916 we wholly relied on French aircraft engines and even by 1918 the shortage of engines was a major brake on the creation of the independent bomber force. Likewise, we relied on European or American sources for all kinds of instruments and gauges, for optical glass, for laboratory equipment, for glass bulbs and tubes for electric lights.

Perhaps the most conspicuous example of British dependence on German industry backed by German education for capability was in drugs and dyes. Whereas Germany was able to switch the largest chemical industry in the world from dyes to explosives and poison gases, Britain had to create a chemical industry almost from scratch in wartime, using confiscated German patents: essentially the birth of ICI. In the case of drugs, however, Britain had to go on covertly importing German products via Switzerland.

Under that most immediate of spurs, the danger of defeat in a great war, the British carried out a veritable industrial revolution to create the advanced industries she had lacked. One might say that the munitions drive of 1914–18 marks the first time that the nation had really accorded top priority to technological success, mobilizing and training its talent accordingly. But the coming of peace saw a swift return to the pre-war pattern. Education for capability continued to lag behind our needs and behind our rivals' efforts; and industry's competitiveness lagged with it. By 1927

British exports had fallen to seventy-three, taking 1913 as 100, while world trade as a whole had risen to 118. The 'practical man' – the *uneducated* practical man, that is – continued to exert his baneful influence on British industry, and on British education. Fundamental education continued to lag. In 1921 only 19 per cent of the population between fourteen and seventeen was in full-time education. In the 1920s generally only 12 per cent of elementary school children went on to secondary, technical or other full-time education. In 1918 Parliament agreed that compulsory part-time education would be introduced for children who left school before eighteen. This has still to come to pass. But in 1924 Germany did introduce such a system. In 1927 a private investigating committee reported on British technical education. It noted the fragmentary nature of the system; the dismally penny-pinched equipment compared with foreign institutions.[15] And in the universities, except for admittedly brilliant original research, science and technology made slow progress between the world wars. Whereas in 1922 there had been 9,852 students in these fields, in 1939 the number had crept up to 10,278. Germany had had 24,000 even before the Great War.

It is therefore not surprising that when we embarked on large-scale re-armament in 1936, the Government found, in the words of the Cabinet Defence Policy and Requirements Committee that 'the most serious factor in the completion of the proposed programme is the limited output of our existing resources.'[16]

The files of this Cabinet Committee fully bear out this gloomy judgement. The British steel industry, for example, remained so fragmented, so old-fashioned, so limited in total output that orders for the armour for the new cruisers and aircraft carriers had to be placed in Czechoslovakia. But the gravest bottle-neck lay in advanced machine-tools for various kinds of precision mass production. From 1933 to 1937, Germany enjoyed nearly 50 per cent of the world's trade in machine-tools; our share was only 7 per cent. Britain therfore had to buy Swiss, German, Hungarian and American machine-tools to enable the re-armament and shadow-factory programme to go forward at all. We had to buy Swiss and American instrumentation for our new aircraft until such times as we could create our manufacture.

Nevertheless the principal bottleneck lay in a shortage of skilled manpower of all kinds, from tool-makers to production managers – which brings us straight back to the question of education for capability. Just as today, there was mass unemployment; and just as today, most of the unemployed were labour useless in advanced technology. In May 1936 the Ministry of Labour reported that the total available unemployed in the engineering industry suitable for precision work numbered 2,000 in the whole country.[17] Time and again in the reports to the Defence Policy and Requirements Committee do we read of the inadequacy of the design departments of companies engaged on re-armament; the lack of production engineers; and the consequent heavy delays and immense muddles in production. That these difficulties were eventually overcome, and that British war production in the Second World War should prove a success story as in the Great War is owing, again as in the Great War, to the fact that under the spur of acute national danger we concentrated supreme effort and all our resources in talent on achieving technological success.

But we must not allow talismans like radar and the Spitfire to blind us to continued shortcomings in bread-and-butter production technology. Professor R.V. Jones writes in his *Most Secret War*[18]:

'They (the Germans) would take simple ideas, and put them straight into practice no matter what technical effort was involved, because they had a far greater command of precision engineering than we had (some notable exceptions such as Rolls Royce apart).'

So we come to the post-war era. Our industrial performance since 1945 is now well known; it follows the pattern set decades earlier, if not a century earlier, and delivers us into our present plight. I believe that antecedent shortcomings in education for capability have acted as one – I don't say the only – key factor in this. But I doubt whether even today we have repaired our century-old backwardness in such education, whether in the primary schools, the secondary schools or in higher and technical education. Even more important, I doubt whether we have yet adjusted the basic values of our society and education in favour of industrial success as a major goal. Until we do this we shall never overcome that pervasive lack of capability, that inferiority of calibre at all levels compared with our rivals, that explain our present want of competitiveness.

Education for capability alone can keep Britain an advanced technological society and save her from becoming a Portugal, perhaps even an Egypt, of tomorrow.

## References

1  Letter to *The Times* by Keith Lockyer, Professor of Operations Management, Management Centre, Bradford University, 10th October, 1975.
2.  *The Engineer in a Changing Society:* address given by John Lyons to the IEE, 10th March, 1977.
3.  BARNETT, C. (1972). *The Collapse of British Power*, London: Methuen, p.95.
4  Ibid.
5  GREAT BRITAIN. HOUSE OF COMMONS. *Report of the Endowed Schools Commission.* Vol. XXXVIII, Part 2 (1867–8), p.72.
6  Cmnd. 3981, p.337.
7  GREAT BRITAIN. HOUSE OF COMMONS. *Report from the Select Committee on Scientific Instruction.* Vol. XV, (1868) p.vi.
8  Ibid.
9  Ibid.
10  Cmnd. 3981, p.20.
11  LOWNDES, G.A.N. (1937). *The Silent Social Revolution.* London: O.U.P., p.89.
12  SANDERSON, M. (1975). *The Universities in the Nineteenth Century.* London: Routledge and Kegan Paul, p.234.
13  *History of the Ministry of Munitions.* Vol. VII, Part II, 1–2.
14  Op. cit., Vol. XII, Part I, p.110.
15  The Emmott Committee Report of an enquiry into the relationship of technical education to other forms of education and to industry and commerce.
16  CAB 16/112, DPR(DR), 9.
17  CAB 16/140, DPR 83.
18  JONES, R.V. (1978). *Most Secret War*, London: Hamish Hamilton, p.230.

# CHAPTER 2
# The Educational Failure
*Patrick Nuttgens*

In the preceding chapter, Correlli Barnett has described Britain's historic failure to prepare its people for the world created by the industrial revolution. This chapter offers an explanation of this specifically educational failure.

The most far-reaching characteristic of education in this country in the last 150 years has been the dislike and fear of technology – and therefore of the modern world. The new technology of the Industrial Revolution was fundamental to that world; it changed the social and economic status quo, upset many conventions of the mind and created the urban and industrial environment of today. Yet, in a rather British way, the attitude of the people developing the educational system was not to exploit it but in some way to correct it, to provide answers to it. In that sense it was a development, not of excitement and wonder, but of fear.

The response was to keep it all under control – so that technology would be subject to civilized values, and designers or inventors discouraged from being too aggressive, all by means of a liberal dose of what Whitehead later called 'inert ideas' – conventional pieces of knowledge and traditional disciplines. Liberal or general studies would make for a balanced education and soften the hard world of technology with a smattering of culture.

It is a central part of my argument that this tradition, so influential and pervasive, was not something inherent or established in the national character, but a direct response, by the intelligentsia, the clergy and the gentry, to the urgent and demanding world of the industrial revolution. It should, after all, have been easy to build upon the fascination with science of the seventeenth century, the spirit of the founders of the Royal Society, the conviction that men were becoming the masters and possessors of nature: or upon the 'enlightenment' of the eighteenth century when men of genius, in Whitehead's words, 'applied the seventeenth century group of scientific abstractions to the analysis of the unbounded universe'. In the event, that excitement became more rarefied, and distinct from the everyday world of technological change. And the mainstream of the intellectual world moved away from the industrial world altogether. It was at heart a retreat, a retreat from reality. And it found its shelter, appropriately, in the cloisters of Oxford. Three figures of nineteenth century Oxford will suffice as representative of the educational ethos. Mark Pattison is usually accepted as the prototype for Mr. Casaubon, the pedant in George Eliot's *Middlemarch*. In fact, Pattison swung between pedantry and a revival of standards of scholarship and teaching at a time when Oxford was badly in need of it. But he remains a symbol – almost the type – of academic scholarship and personal remoteness, obsessed with and utterly absorbed by the minutiae of the intellectual life.

More creatively Newman represents – and in his *Idea of a University* specifically sets out – ideals of university education, and thus of education as a whole. Central to that approach was the idea of education as an end in itself, untouched at its highest and best by having to make a thing or earn a living: 'the intellect, instead of being formed or sacrificed to some particular or accidental purpose, some specific trade or profession, or study or science, is disciplined for its own sake, for the perception of its own proper object, and for its own higher culture . . .'

But the most immediately influential statement establishing the ethos of an educated and cultured élite dominating the whole field of learning and society was Matthew Arnold's *Culture and Anarchy*. Arnold's influence was wide; he was, after all, both an academic and, for most of his career, an inspector of schools. The book, as he later remarked, was one of the only books to have become a classic in the lifetime of its author; and that was because Arnold found words to give his readers an instant recognition of the intellectual issues of their time. For him and them, anarchy was the world of industry and machines and therefore of dehumanization; culture was the corrective, the answer to it; and the signs of culture were sweetness and light. For culture 'does not try to teach down to the level of inferior classes; it does not try to win them for this or that sect of its own, with ready-made judgements and watchwords. It seeks to do away with classes; to make the best that has been thought and known in the world current everywhere; to make all men live in an atmosphere of sweetness and light, where they may use ideas, as it uses them itself, freely-nourished and not bound by them'.

With one great intellectual leap, Arnold established the ethos of the middle classes and did so in the same decade as Forster's Education Act. It was of course a help in becoming a man of culture if you had a reasonable income already or earned one on the side; but what was clear was that the act of making, a deep involvement in design and technology, could not be a route to culture. The great divide between enlightenment and work was now designated and preserved.

Those three intellectual expositors, even the many people influenced by them, could not however have established such a complete and lasting outfit of social and educational values if their work has not been reinforced by a conscious or unconscious acceptance of a profound philosophical system. What underlay that intellectual movement was the thought of Plato, and specifically the revival of his thought in the neo-Platonism of the nineteenth century. It is difficult to exaggerate the importance of this intellectual substratum. It affected in the most fundamental way the entire educational world. And it still does.

For the profound attraction of Plato's thought was precisely to offer the intellectual an escape from the mundane world of everyday work and living. Reality was not in that world; reality was in the world of Forms or Ideas, to which the everyday world was a more or less successful approximation. It was a wonderful piece of sleight of mind, turning things upside down and finding the most respectable philosophical justification for the privileged world of leisure, discussion and speculation, a pure world of clear and perfect unities not to be found in the imperfect, flawed and confused world of industry and work.

Plato is the ultimate authority for the nineteenth and twentieth century concept, or ideal, of a liberal education. He was not responsible for its gaining a stranglehold upon the system. It did so because it neatly fitted the hierarchical character of British society.

A liberal education became the peak to which an education should aspire. The ordinary mind dealt with things; the educated mind dealt in ideas. It had a profound effect upon the most influential institutions.

There seem to be periods in the life of all institutions when their leaders become so self-concerned that they turn in upon themselves and concentrate upon their own self-improvement and self-preservation rather than the service they do to the outside world. Society may now and again hammer upon the door and shout for them to come and lend a hand in the street. Mostly there is no answer. Withdrawal from everyday affairs is a constant temptation of the academic world, usually in the universities, today probably in the polytechnics; everyday realities are so much less simple than the contemplation of eternal truths.

And where better to contemplate them than in the universities, first the ancient and wealthy colleges of Oxford and Cambridge, then in the civic universities, founded as colleges for practical training and quickly celebrating their admission into the higher world of learning. Increasingly, with every year, through the nineteenth and twentieth centuries, the universities and the university ethos came to dominate the whole of education. They were the peak; they set the standard; and they were a magic world to which the fortunate might one day be admitted.

To make sure of this and fill a gap that might have remained in the circle of education, the Government took a decision in 1917 that was to have the most permanent and drastic effect upon the fortunes of the country. In that year the Government, in an attempt to tidy up and give some order to the chaos of school-leaving examinations, decreed that the universities would be responsible for conducting school-leaving examinations. The system was now complete. For, although it was emphasized by the Board of Education that it should be 'a cardinal principle that the examinations should follow a curriculum and not determine it', in practice the very opposite happened.

The examinations and their requirements became the key to studies in secondary schools. They were supposed to be school-leaving examinations: they inevitably became qualifying examinations for entry to the universities. This profoundly affected the orientation of studies and teaching. It made entry to the universities the highest aspiration for teachers and pupils, and thus had a profound bearing upon the subjects which would be taught, their nature and scope, and the character of the educational experience of the pupils.

For it followed from that simple decision that the ethos of the university should become fundamental to the whole of education and training. And what did the universities deal in? Not training for a job, not developing skills in design and making, not encouraging action: they dealt in learning, grouped into subjects and disciplines and neatly compartmented according to the subject rather than the needs of people or society.

So education became the assembly of subjects and then, at the higher level, disciplines. They, like Platonic forms, had their own essence; they were to be handed on, or such parts of them as seemed reasonable to communicate. And what kept them in good shape was more and more study of them, becoming more specialized with every year and eventually, under the influence of Germany and America, receiving the delectable accolade of research. The academic factory was now in business, sufficient unto itself; research, including literary research about matters so uninteresting that no one was likely to want to do it again, became the aim of the learned. Among that research a small proportion was of the utmost significance for the future of the world. But for the most part, the material just poured in and out, weighing down the library floor, becoming sooner or later itself the stuff for more research and more papers. This tradition, and especially the conventional acceptance of 'inert knowledge', is so general and established that it still inspires and under-lies almost all educational thinking. Its pervasiveness can be seen in the official summary of the 'Great Debate' on education, published as a green paper under the title *Education in Schools: A Consultative Document*. It is a document remarkable for its conventionality, its lack of ideas and its profound complacence. It is of course orientated towards educational administration and politics rather than teaching. But what is particularly fascinating is the list of aims of the schools which 'the majority of people would probably agree with'. Out of eight wordy aims, only one contains, in a phrase tacked on at the end, 'giving them the ability . . . to apply themselves to tasks' – a hint that it might be good for children to learn to do something. There is a reference to engaging in work in primary schools as part of the 'child-centred' approach; but generally education is seen to need more standard assessment and an agreed secondary curriculum for all pupils. And what that education really consists of is information, critical discussion and appreciation of such estimable things as the mixed economy, the political system and the wealth creating parts of industry.

Supporting it all is the substratum of conventional accepted values. The gifted will go on to academic studies; the less gifted should turn their attention to careers and the world of work, presumably earning enough to keep the gifted in study. There is no hint that it might be good for the gifted to enter work, and not even a suspicion that there might be something to be said for learning to do things, to make things, to invent, to wonder, to discover the fascination of nature and things, and the fantastic possibilities in doing and making. Even though it is familiar knowledge that you must start it early if you want to cultivate a habit or a skill or an attitude, it seems to have been forgotten that the conventional kind of schooling might be re-examined, to ask at least if there might be a more real and fundamental way of learning to take part in an urban industrial society than just to add to the curriculum a few classes on appreciation.

The one imaginative attempt to do something about this, after the Second World War, is now usually treated to an embarrassed silence. The Secondary Modern experiment had to fail, for three reasons. The teachers and administrators responsible for it were so shaped by conventional education that they could not in practice carry the experiment right through, with all its implications for teaching and learning; there was no recognized and respected sector of higher education to which they could be related and which was necessary to give continuity and status; and they fitted only too easily into a low-level niche in our deeply divisive hierarchical society, instead of making a bridge and a new practical reality.

There is, in Britain, a deeply ingrained belief that practical people must be stupid. It is a belief that will not be changed by the creation of mixed ability classes in comprehensive schools. It is still assumed that the brighter will go on to further study and the dimmer will do practical tasks. But that rests upon two basic assumptions: that the brighter will always want to move away from work, and that brightness is of a certain kind; that is, verbal and numerical. We are trapped in a net of conventional ideas about brightness or cleverness. What is required is a radical reassessment of what we mean by cleverness and stupidity. In an advanced technological society there should be different ways of grading cleverness and stupidity.

There is a fundamental connection between living and learning. The start of education is in living. Much of it subsequently is affected by the process of learning as well as by its content. We know this from our own experience, and in our primary schools we act on the knowledge that doing and learning are intimately related.

What happens? That wonderful mixture of life, learning, family, fun, playing and studying comes at the beginning. At its best, it is not just permissiveness or lack of discipline, but a controlled unity of living and learning. But there is a dramatic change as soon as the pupils enter secondary education. The schools are bigger; that enables them to have better facilities and a wider range of subjects for 'A' levels as well as more money for the headmaster. But the change is more fundamental than that.

It is a change to another mode of learning. For now it is a world of handed-down culture, of information, of exercises that become increasingly sophisticated, a world that revolves around the teaching of generalizations: principles, rules, laws, probabilities. In terms of scholarship that may well be right, But in human terms, teaching has been turned upside down. Where previously the pupil's own experience led towards the forming of generalizations, now generalizations are followed by practice and then, with any luck, lead back to experience. The classroom takes the place of the studio or workshop. And that is where the status race begins. The brightest are those who respond most easily to this mode of learning; the dimmest are those who learn from doing and making. In fact, it is a circular situation. The secondary system discovers the brightest children. The brightest children are those who are discovered by the secondary system. By the age of thirteen or fourteen we have already divided them into those moving towards learning and those moving towards work.

## Learning to Some Purpose

In this chapter I have tried to explain Britain's long-standing educational failure, rooted in the status ranking of subjects and activities. It seems to me clear that what we need is greater variety: high standards with different curricula rather than uniform curricula with different standards. We need more change, more freedom, so as to create education for capability. Capability involves not only thinking and analysing but the ability to make and to do – and the ability to do what you say you will do. This means righting the imbalance of our educational world. It suggests a change in the way education is divided and subdivided, into subjects and disciplines. It is not the content but the division of knowledge which is obsolete and stultifying. If we are serious about education, we must deal with activities rather than subjects, with courses rather than disciplines: we need a radical regrouping of knowledge and action. The subjects should not be ends in themselves as they are now; they should be means to an end – understanding and action, work and satisfaction. Such a regrouping is known in practice. As soon as you try to apply advanced knowledge or research to practical affairs, you have to cross academic boundaries and remove the barriers of conventional disciplines.

Another removable obstacle is an assumption which starts in the secondary schools and grows from that point: that education is ultimately for the isolated and unique individual self. The whole curriculum is devised to that end: self-recognition, self-awareness, self-expression. It is so common that it is taken for granted. But it stems from a particular cultural and philosophical tradition and needs to be seriously questioned. It was challenged by John Macmurray in his Gifford lectures of 1953 and 1954, from which I quote only two sentences as an indication of a major work of original thinking:

> 'The isolated, purely individual self is a fiction in philosophy. This means . . . that the unity of the personal cannot be thought as the form of an individual self, but only through the mutuality of personal relationship'.

The problem of status only disappears when people are working constructively and effectively together towards a common end which is outside themselves. Paradoxically that gives a new dimension to their own experience and their own personalities. That is the ultimate lesson for education.

We are at the end of the era to which our conventional educational system belongs. The new one, which is also of course a very old one, must be inspired by a recognition of the central importance of everyman and of mutuality. The challenge is to discover a more rewarding education in which thinking and doing and making are fused into a new concept of living and learning.

# CHAPTER 3
# The New Industrial Society

*Charles Handy*

## Introduction

In Chapter 1 Correlli Barnett discussed the reasons for Britain's
low level of productivity compared with her rival countries and the
low priority given to industry by our educational and social
traditions. Both of these challenges are real, urgent and critical.

This chapter looks forward, to the long-term future of our
industrial society. This society will see big changes, and those
changes will demand new responses from our educational system.
Capability will become even more necessary, in certain very
particular ways.

One change will be in employment. Within the next thirty years,
when today's secondary school pupils are at the peak of their
careers, it may be as odd to hear someone speak of being
'employed' as it is today to hear someone describe themselves as
being 'in service' (domestic service).

I grew up in a country vicarage which was thought to be
unmanageable without two girls in service and a full-time
gardener; and we were poor folk, impoverished gentry. But
yesterday's 'unthinkable' becomes tomorrow's commonplace.
That vicarage still stands and runs quite well, without its servants.

We must watch out for these changes in language. They are
often the bugles of social drama, the outward and visible signs of a
more stealthy but deep-seated social change: a social paradigm
shift. 'Paradigm' was a word made fashionable by T.S. Kuhn when
describing famous revolutions in scientific thinking. A paradigm is
a conceptual framework, a way of looking at the world, a set of
assumed premises into which we pile the facts. When Copernicus

suggested that the earth was not at the centre of the Universe he was, though he knew it not, a paradigm revolutionary. We are about to enter on a time of paradigm shifts in the world of work. That does not mean that work will not get done, that industry will not exist, or that wealth will not get created. The planets continued their motion unworried by Copernicus. It was the minds of men which changed. The way they now viewed their earth in the full scheme of things had profound effects on their values, beliefs and behaviour. Similarly domestic chores still get done today in my vicarage, but differently. Work, industry, commerce, government: they will all still get done under the new paradigm, but differently. It is the difference that will make the difference to all of us, but most particularly to those concerned with educating the inheritors of the new future.

Paradigm changes, like all changes, are most vigorously resisted by those currently at the centre of things. Quite naturally–when you have eventually mastered your world you do not want the ground rules to change until you, at least, have ended your time. Selective perception then becomes a great prop to the *status quo* as we see only that which we want to see and overlook the inconvenient. Thus it is that new paradigms creep in from the edges and are often best perceived by those on the fringes of things, even if, like Cassandra, their heralds are only understood after the event. Cassandra saw only trauma. I see a new dawn after a gloomy night.

My first suggestion is that two important formulae which have governed our lives in the industrialized countries are coming to the end of their useful life. They have proved to have the seeds of their own destruction within them as we enter the post-scarcity society. The first of these formulae is: **Concentration + Specialization = Efficiency.**

The second, which is connected to the first, is that: **Economic Wealth = Success.**

These formulae have served us very well in the past two hundred years. The invention of the joint-stock company, then of limited liability and then, ten years later, of the idea that companies could own other companies, gave us a head start in the benefits of concentration. When factories replaced sheds for gangs, technology added its weight to finance. Concentrate, then specialize. That way you got the economies of scale which pulled down costs, made yesterday's luxuries today's commonplaces and made 'production' the servant of the consumer society. Management became in effect the art or science of *co-ordinating specialization within appropriate concentration*, and thus was scarcity eliminated. What real poverty that now exists in industrialized societies is the result of ineffectual or unfair distribution, not of scarcity. This principle of concentration plus efficiency was sensed to be so powerful that it was carried far beyond industry into other areas of society, including government and, most recently, education.

But there is a flaw in the formula, or rather there are two flaws. Specialization demands specialists, and today we are all specialists whether we have a degree or a union card to prove it. Respectable specialists belong to professions and have associations. Less respectable ones have closed shops. The difference is often only semantic. Now this desirable combination of concentration and specialization has produced those tightly designed organizations which are the joy of the organizational draughtsman in which every cog in the machine has a vital part to play: excellent, until one of those cogs seizes up, in which case the whole machine grinds to a halt. We see the effect of the tight-designed organization often enough today, for various groups of specialists have come to see that if they can organize themselves they have in fact been granted *hi-jack power* in the enterprise. The principle of concentration yields ripe plums to any selfish specialist, for in the short-term it nearly always pays to buy off the hi-jackers.

And why would the specialists not be selfish? It is hard for we humans to identify with groups where (a) we do not know everyone at least by face, and (b) we have no power, formal or informal, to influence events. Concentration requires unit sizes and methods of co-ordination where both of these conditions are impossible. In any case, it often does not matter because concentration usually results in a limited monopoly so that increased costs can be passed on as increased prices. There are limits of course: when no-one rides the trains or posts a letter or buys a British car, one might re-consider. Even then 'we have our methods', including import controls. But the flaw in the formula is that it must ultimately self-destruct for purely economic reasons unless productivity increases *always* exceed inflation (that is, the benefits of the formula exceed its costs) which has *never* happened over any period in any industrialized nation.

But there is one other flaw: a psychological one as opposed to an economic one. Specialization means limitation: one applies one's talents, energies and knowledge to a defined area. Marvellous if you are a medical consultant or a professor, or an R & D type where there are unplumbed depths to explore within that small plot you have chosen or been given. Every day can be new even though your focus is unchanged. But try digging a plot when there is concrete one foot down – and all around. It does get boring – even alienating. Specialization *has* to be defined and confined if the benefits of concentration are to be achieved. In the heyday of concentration and specialization, in Detroit in the 1960s, one car assembly plant had a labour turnover rate of 70 per cent per annum. When I asked whether this did not mean a huge training operation I was told 'no', they had so broken down the jobs that *anyone* off the street could be trained in one hour and twenty minutes. They saw no connection between their two statistics.

Things are better now, but it does not make much difference if the concrete is two feet down instead of one, the job-cycle eighteen minutes instead of nine. Absenteeism in Britain accounts for *100 times* more days lost than industrial disputes. In France their *average* worker takes twenty-four days per annum in absenteeism and sick leave. In Scandinavia it is even more. That is another straight 10 per cent on the wage bill apart from the inconvenience. And it is not getting any better.

Let us turn to the second formula: **Economic Wealth = Success.** With suitable genuflections to the quality of life, all of us, and certainly all political parties, subscribe to this formula for the nation. We may dispute how the wealth should be distributed; indeed we do, quite bitterly, but we all agree that there should be more of it. It is this formula that activates the first, the link being the equation **Efficiency = Economic Wealth.** Once again, however, there is a flaw, still small enough to need a microscope but growing every day. For the formula that worked so well when we all needed to work to live loses a lot of its point when scarcity is conquered. Professor Fred Hirsch argued in his book *The Social Limits to Growth* that we now work increasingly for positional goods, goods that in some way set us apart from others. The hope is that these positional goods are always changing, for as soon as everyone has, say, a television set, it is of no use as a positional good unless it is perhaps a television set in your car! When anyone can join your club you might as well leave it. Like Groucho Marx, why would I want to join a club which admits people like me? Education, of course, has long been a positional good: in many countries you buy into it through fees or through a house in the right catchment area. The problem is that positional goods and proper democracy do not sit easily together. If economic growth is fuelled by people looking for positional goods you will have a society in which a minority is always envied by a majority. You will certainly achieve economic growth, but you will also get social divisiveness, relative deprivation, unrest and even revolution. When economic wealth meant survival the envy of the poor for the rich could be contained and efficiency guaranteed. When economic wealth, in a post-scarcity age, means television in the car, two homes and private education, for some but not for others, then the demands of efficiency seem less palatable.

Who wants all these positional goods anyway? Not the British, apparently. In a *New Society* poll in 1977, 80 per cent of the respondents said they would not work harder or longer even if they had the chance of significantly more money. Young Germans, too, according to another poll, prefer more time and more personal freedom to more money. But time and personal freedom are not positional; everyone can have as much of them as he wants without depreciating their value for others.

Economic wealth, then, as it relates to national success, may be one of those graphs that level out at a certain point: the post-scarcity stage. We do not want our wealth to drop: maybe it should rise a little, but the costs of increasing it significantly and continuously are beginning, in the eyes of many, to outweigh its benefits. Success needs to be redefined.

**The New Paradigm**

We need a new paradigm, a paradigm in which the ingredients of efficiency and success are redefined. In thirty years' time that paradigm will be clear. Children then will look back on the age of industrial capitalism with, I fancy, puzzlement. They will, if they are wise, recognize its great achievement. Under the old paradigm scarcity was conquered, many millions were dragged out of a life of deprivation and squalor, and the foundations were built for a new hope for man. It is a paradigm that can still be useful in many lands for many years until, as with us now, its costs begin to outweigh its benefits. We can see clues to the new paradigm although its final shape must remain hidden for a while yet. Let me suggest some of the unnoticed clues which I believe I can see. If I am even half-right, they are clues to the world for which we are *today* educating our younger children.

## The Communications Revolution

The principle of concentration had it that you pulled everything into the centre and then pushed it out again. Rationalization used to mean closing depots and any outlying bits. This procedure may well go into reverse. The costs of physical transport will almost certainly go on rising faster than other costs, partly because there is no practical alternative to fossil fuel in transport for at least fifty years and fossil fuel is bound to get even more expensive as supplies run out; and partly because the limits of size and specialization have already been reached in physical transport. On the other hand, *electronic* communication systems are getting cheaper, more relevant and more adaptable every day. As communication over ground gets more expensive, communication through the air gets ever cheaper. There will soon be very strong *economic* arguments for disaggregating *physical* manufacture but linking it electronically to central design and control facilities. 'Kits' will become very sophisticated, so that garages will assemble whole cars, and communities, small fertilizer plants. Mobile factories or automatic factories will become more commonplace, so that, for instance, you could buy your spectacles from a self-operated manufacturing machine, not unlike a xerox or a photography booth. The technology is there; it only needs a reverse in communications economics to make it practicable.

**Fees not Wages**

There is a difference between work and employment, and between fees and wages. Professionals charge *fees* for *work* done. Employees are paid *wages* for *time* spent (which should result in work done). As the costs and problems of employment rise (to employers) it will become increasingly common to contract out as much work as possible to independent individuals or groups. If Marks and Spencer can contract out their manufacturing side and still control it, so can others even if it is technically more complex. If hamburger chains can sell their wares by a franchising system, employing no-one, so can others. If small traders can contract out their accounting work to independents, so can large traders, particularly now that electronics mean that you do not have to let go control of quantity or quality when you let go of the work. Increasingly, people will say, 'I *do* work for someone' rather than 'I work for someone'; and they will do it for fees rather than wages.

**Small is Necessary**

Small is not always beautiful, but a sense of appropriate size is becoming more common. Regions are preferred to counties, towns to cities. Economics again comes to the aid of human inclinations. The costs of co-ordination and administration are now seen to escalate disproportionately with size, partly due to the flaws in the first formula. The point of diminishing returns comes sooner and sooner. For instance, there are new bio-chemical processes for making protein out of vegetable wastes, but they are uneconomic if anything has to be carried for more than twenty miles or stored too long. This will help to set optimum limits (from the point of view of food costs) to conurbations. Just as medieval towns were limited to 30,000 people for hundreds of years because that was the number which could be fed by the countryside within a day's reach of a wagon, so tomorrow's towns may be limited to the number who can live off the vegetable wastes generated by a twenty mile radius.

But there is another pressure towards smallness. In work organizations authority is becoming increasingly personal. People

EC–D

do not obey, they agree. Some call it the decline of deference, others the rise of individuality (it depends which side you're on!) The practical effect is that you cannot lead or influence people in organizations unless you can relate to them personally, and that puts an effective limit on unit size. It may be 200, it may be 500. But it certainly is not 5000. Eighty-five per cent of Britons, in one survey, would like to live in a village. They may be fantasizing about village life, but they are also saying something about the appropriate size of communities.

**Tools not Machines**

The advent of the micro-processor has already begun to turn machines back into tools. Man is the master of his tools but the servant of his machine. The industrial jig is turning the factory worker into a craftsman. It also permits a sort of high technology do-it-yourself. The home computer may be a positional good today but it will eventually become an indispensable aid to any budding craftsman whether he works for love or for gain. The high technology tool will make possible a return to out-work and piece-rates at a new level of sophistication: work done instead of time spent, again. These tools will allow many people to become arbiters of their own destinies in their work as well as their private lives. The more sophisticated tools will no doubt be grouped in some common location so that they can be appropriately serviced and maintained – a new kind of sophisticated equipment hire operation. The models are already there: technology will transfer them.

**The Economics of Quality**

Money may be necessary, but it is for many no longer the ultimate criterion now that scarcity is no longer the ogre that it was. Both in personal and in national calculations the non-material aspects of life are becoming included in the calculations of success. More people realize that to value non-renewable resources in the same way as renewable resources is to mortgage our children's future. More people feel that to define wealth or GNP to include our overcrowded commuter trains, the cost of motorway accidents, and the provision of more arms, prisons and policemen is crazy economics. The OECD already puts together an alternative calculation with the unappealing title of Net National Welfare Index which includes more qualitative facts. The Japanese use a similar index for their long-term planning, although there is as yet little indication of its effect in that country.

There are other ways of defining growth than by material consumption. Personal time and liberty, the creative arts, the literacy level, the incidence of crime, the rate of suicide, mental illness, alcholism; all of these could be the ingredients of a new international league table which might more closely approximate to what people *already* feel.

The idea of a social wage is already a reality. Many people today feel *entitled* to money to live on because they have been born into a society. We already live in a pocket-money economy where essentials are provided and we work for the extras. If you grow up with that feeling of entitlement money *is* less important.

### The Consequences

Rooted as we are today in our tried and tested formulae for efficiency and success, all these clues to a new pattern of work and society must seem like pipe-dreams. Staunch paradigm-defenders will deplore, or scoff at, much of it. The older amongst them may be safe to do so for paradigm changes do not happen overnight. The two paradigms – the old and the new – will march beside each other for many years, causing great discomfort and uncertainty to society. I have aimed my sights thirty years ahead, a generation hence, when today's secondary school pupils are in mid-life. That's a long way off for some; it is awfully near for those who are educating our boys and girls today. Deploring the emerging paradigm or applauding it, I would claim, is rather akin to discussing the British weather: you may have ample material for a dinner-table argument but nothing you say will change the weather. The clues are there, I am sure, in the conflux of economics, technology and social forces. We can only argue about whence they lead, and the possible consequences.

I see all sorts of consequences. Organizations will become much more dispersed, becoming federations of small semi-autonomous villages. Many of the villagers will be self-employed, except that employment will not be a common word; contract will be the thing. Communities, regions, even countries will tend to become more self-sufficient (partly because of the increased cost of transport). Temporary tariff barriers to allow home industries to get started will be negotiated between regions and countries more readily. Towns will grow, and cities will shrink. People will travel in big hops or little hops, with not much in between. Individuals will tend to have specialist careers rather than organizational careers: chemical engineers, not ICI; fitters, not British Leyland. They will look for support not to employers (or to unions against employers) but to professional or trade associations (the new rôle for the unions?) With a social wage and self-employment, words like unemployment, retirement and redundancy will be as inappropriate to many workers as they are today to housewives, who work harder than any of us. Those who do contract their full-time energies to an organization will do so for finite periods (five to ten years) and most will find few such opportunities after forty-five years of age. As a nation we shall increasingly move out of labour-intensive industries for *export* into know-how exports in which there is a high added value for expertise. The City, technical consultancy, specialist cars and other products, high-technology manufacture, education, all fit this know-how category. But there should be a return to self-sufficiency in all countries in the more basic goods and commodities. It will increasingly be ridiculous to import wire shopping baskets from West Germany (as we now do) when transport costs escalate and once we realize that a new form of cottage industry can make such things very easily.

There is an optimistic and a pessimistic viewpoint on all of this. The optimist can envisage a thriving manufacturing industry with the constraint of maintaining unemployment removed; an industry well capable of supporting the infrastructure of a pocket-money economy, if it has moved into the high-added value export field. The number of jobs in manufacturing industry will fall as dramatically as those in agriculture did in the earlier industrial revolution, but this should release talent for the so-called tertiary sector: the services, education, and leisure activities. Indeed, with many of the pressures of a materialist paradigm removed, work could be re-defined to include all creative activity whether done for money or not. Communities should develop again as they become more self-contained and personal mobility diminishes. Bureaucracy will no doubt thrive, particularly the legal and quasi-legal bits; but if contained within regions and communities it may at least have a human face. Sport, the arts, the caring professions, and family life may all have their heyday as man discovers there is more to this life than material wealth.

The pessimist (which probably means most Britons) will have no Utopias. To him the new paradigm seems designed for that small band of self-sufficient middle-class professionals, used to carving out their own careers and life-styles. He envisages an army of dependent layabouts living on their social wage, desperate for the modern variety of bread and circuses, growing obese in front of their television sets in human battery coops, with successive governments trying to extract more and ever more from the 'productive' sector to buy off these indolent voters. When bribes fail, as they always do, governments will perforce turn to other forms of social control, including not only regulations but the mass media, education and, perhaps, religion.

Optimism or pessimism? Can we turn the inevitable into the desirable? This, to me, is the challenge to all of us who have charge of shaping the minds, hearts and hands of the young and the not so young. Economics, technology and an amalgam of social forces will, as I see it, set new rules for the game of life in the next century. Education will provide the players. Steeped in the traditions of one game, we must prepare players for the next.

# PART TWO:
# Towards Solutions

## In General

## In Particular

# CHAPTER 4
# Implications for Education
*Charles Handy*

The implications for education of the emerging world which I have described in the last chapter are urgent and profound. I suggest that the basis for a new education must be self-sufficiency and community. In short, what is needed is not so much a change in organization, curriculum or pedagogy as a fundamental revision of attitudes which makes inevitable a revision of the system. It is always convenient to blame things on the system. It removes from one the obligation to do anything oneself, for *others* are always responsible for the system. We shall come back to that, for I submit that systems are, in this land, changed best by conspicuous experiment turned proven case law.

I have three prejudices; none very new but given new urgency by the emerging shape of the new society of work. I am deeply prejudiced against:

(a)  the primacy of knowledge in our system;
(b)  the institutionalization of learning;
(c)  the age-bonding of education.

Let me explain briefly.

## The Primacy of Knowledge

Do we owe to the Greek philosophers, to the ideal of all-knowing Renaissance man or to the tradition of Mr. Arnold, the view that he who knows all can do all and be all? Whatever its origins, the notion that the head guides the hands and the hearts has dominated our educational tradition for the past 150 years or so. The slopes of Parnassus, as John Locke pointed out, are not the best training grounds for the world.

The primacy of knowledge in our educational tradition did allow for one uniform approach to education with an internal self-validating set of criteria. If everyone is doing X then success can safely be measured in terms of X irrespective of its effects on Y. As long as you fiddle beautifully, so the message seems to go, it matters not that Rome burns.

I am not arguing here for a fully vocational approach to education or denying that some things should be studied because they are good in themselves. I am only pointing out that by adopting knowledge as the universal and self-validating criterion of success in education the British people have been able to avoid many inconvenient questions for many years.

The changes in society that I see coming will make these questions even more intrusive than they already are. It is not that knowledge and the creation of knowledge will cease to be important; indeed, their importance will increase in a know-how world, but the skills, crafts and arts of making, doing and being will have to be made legitimate. Schools are the advance guards, the heralds of society, and it is here that the signs must be made clear to the youth of the new age.

It is, I know, easier to preach than to practise when you are locked into a system based on the primacy of knowledge. I will return to that.


### The Institutionalization of Learning

We have a habit, when a problem is inconvenient, of locking it up in a building with the words 'Institute of' in front of the name of the problem (as with Race Relations, Crime Prevention, Housing, etc.). It does not actually solve the problem but it absolves the rest of us from caring about it. I sometimes think that we have done this with learning – we have locked the problem up in 'Schools' and then felt free to go about our business. It was John Rae of Westminster School whom I heard once remark on the radio that the 1944 Education Act was a confidence trick in that it suggested to parents that the State and its schools would take care of the education of their children. Any of us who have been involved in formal education at any level would be happy to admit to a greater humility.

Many of us would, I suspect, like to see formal learning spread more thinly throughout life and dispersed more widely in the community. No school can be a microcosm of life. No school should try to be. With the best will in the world they are institutions – and closed institutions at that, custodial if you like. Such institutions are inevitably about rules and the maintenance of rules; they are about dependency and its obverse counterdependency. I grew up in those institutions, and whatever else I learnt, I learnt only one way to relate to authority, to adults and to institutions. It took me a long time to outgrow my basic passivity, obedience and, I think, distrust in the face of any authority. And they were, I think, good schools that I attended.

We have forgotten the values of apprenticeship. Not only is apprenticeship the best known way of learning craft skills, or such attributes as judgement, precision, patience and self-discipline, it is an excellent way of learning to work with adults.

Self-sufficiency (the key requirement of the new society) is an acquired habit. Recent research on that creature of our age, the international manager, has demonstrated that a capability to adapt to new cultures, scenes and systems is a key element in success. Keats called it a 'negative capability', the capacity to contain uncertainty. This capability is greatly enhanced if, in youth, the individual has experienced several changes of scene with success: culture-changing as inoculation for life. Of course the injection can be worse than the disease if it is not carefully managed. Good families do it well, as long as they are not too protective. Schools by definition cannot do it within their own system. One enclosed environment is a bad preparation for multiple open environments in later life.

I am arguing for devices such as work-experience schemes, for transferable credits between schools, for more classes linked to facilitating outside experiences, for qualification systems that allow other forms of competence recognition besides examinations, for certificates of experience, for craft schools tied to work-places.

I should, in short, like to see schools supplement families as the centres of learning networks, rather than as closed institutions. I know that some will fall through the gaps. I know we shall need new and different staff. I plead only that an uncoupled system of learning will be a much better proving-ground for an uncoupled society. Institutionalized learning may have suited an institutional society. It will soon be very out-of-date and counter-productive.


**The Age-Bonding of Education**

If education and learning are to be dispersed more widely through the community they must also be spread more thinly through life. We all know that the Anglo-Saxon preference for getting rid of education as early as possible is quite absurd. The spectacle of middle-class parents spending huge fortunes to get their children through 'A' levels before their neighbours' still strikes me as one of the saddest steeplechases around.

Why are we felt to have failed if we have not passed a certain grade by a certain age? Examinations often do not test competence, but age-related performance. Who wants that? When youth is paid the same as experience why should any one buy youth? Why is it so hard to get back into the qualifications game if you take two years off to gain experience? All of these questions are going to become much more acute in the new society.

The new patterns of work will make it essential that school and work (call them by what names you will) interleave throughout life. Technical qualifications will increasingly have an effective expiry date. Entrance to contracts will be increasingly dependent on valid certificates of competence. The delights of the humanities will increasingly be sought after by the middle-aged who scorned them in their teens.

My forecast would be that we shall see an increase in qualifications but they will be less tied to institutions and to age. Rather as with music examinations, you will take them when you are ready for them, with the examining and certifying bodies moving *farther* away from the institutions. Professions, semi-professions and craft unions will set increasingly formal requirements and specialized schools will grow up to prepare people for their examinations, many of them taking the place of sixth-form colleges.

This new proliferation of educational paths and gateways would be welcomed by me. It will, however, seem like a maze to the uninitiated. Choice sounds great until you realize that choice comes accompanied by responsibility. The career counselling services will no doubt have a boom; let us hope they are prepared for it.

## Conclusion

One theory of learning holds that all learning is a sequence of three questions: What? So what? Now what? I have tried to answer the 'What?' and 'So what?' The 'Now what?' remains.

I do not believe that the kind of changes which I see as necessary and indeed as, eventually, inevitable will happen by decree from the centre. The law and the system move to ratify the existing state of affairs. Change happens as experiment succeeds experiment until the experiments become case-law and the consensus has subtly shifted.

If this theory of change is accepted we need more *conspicuous experiments*. One of the deficiencies of a closed system is that experiments are not encouraged, indeed are seen as deviations, rebellions or eccentricities. My defence of a private sector in anything, be it health, education or even policing, is that it should be the experimental sector, rewarded with the fruits of successful risk-taking as well as the penalties of mistakes. I would plead therefore for more experiments, for more publicity, for interesting experiments, for more encouragement from educational authorities for experiment, for a licence to take risks.

From my knowledge of the educational world I can say that there is no shortage of ideas or schemes. Indeed, all that I have said here is old-hat by many standards. What seems to be lacking is the freedom to experiment. Those of us who are concerned with 'Education for Capability' are anxious to do what we can to create a climate for *appropriate* experiment and to do anything possible to help with such experiments. This chapter has been one attempt to define what we mean by 'appropriate' in the context of the future shape of industry and patterns of work in our society.

# CHAPTER 5
# Education: for what?
*Toby Weaver*

In this chapter, I should like to attempt to describe the broad capacities and attributes that have been taken to constitute the armoury or equipment of the educated man or woman, and the motives which impel people to seek them. In the light of the earlier discussion I shall try to identify six attributes which, if they were combined in high degree and appropriate balance in any one person, would represent educational excellence.

The first centres on that ambiguous word 'culture': ambiguous, because the social scientist uses it descriptively, the humanist prescriptively. In the former sense it was defined more than eighty years ago as 'that complex whole which includes knowledge, belief, art, morals, law, custom and any other capabilities and habits acquired by man as a member of society'; or, more recently, as 'a concept that refers in a general sense to the designs for adapting to the social and physical environments which characterize the life of a particular population'. It was in this sense, I think, that the Robbins Committee postulated the transmission of a common culture and common standards of citizenship as one of the four objectives of higher education. On this view the educated man is one who has been initiated (or socialized as it is now being called) into his cultural heritage, and habituated to the ways of behaving prevalent in his society.

For the educator culture has a further, normative, meaning. 'Culture', says Whitehead, 'is activity of thought and receptiveness to beauty and humane feeling.' 'Culture', says Matthew Arnold, 'is, or ought to be, the study and pursuit of perfection; and that, of perfection as pursued by culture, beauty and intelligence, or, in other words, sweetness and light are the main characters.' In this sense it is frequently hymned as the pursuit of excellence and symbolizes the quintessence of a liberal or humanistic education. It has always been a central strand in the higher education tradition which sees the universities and the schools that serve them as, at their best, sanctuaries of culture and nurseries of character. While few people claim to know how, and some people doubt whether this aspiration can be effectively embodied through institutional means in the lives of learners, it remains true that educators have valued it highly as both process and achievement under the name of **Cultivation.**

A second prominent education aim, akin to but distinguishable from the first, has been the transmission to the learner of knowledge and understanding as ends in themselves. This is at the heart of the academic tradition. Its watchword is the pursuit of truth for its own sake as an intrinsic value. Its proponents see the definitive characteristic of *homo sapiens* as residing in his mind or intellect. You will be familiar with its prophets. 'That perfection of the intellect, which is the result of education and its beau ideal', wrote Newman, 'to be imparted to individuals in their respective measures, is the clear, calm, accurate vision and comprehension of all things, as far as the finite mind can embrace them.' It is reflected, too, in Mark Pattison's vision of the *totum scribile.* Of the effort to achieve a grasp of the whole span of human knowledge, 'This is the life', he wrote, 'that the higher education aspires to promote.'

The same emphasis is to be found in the Robbins Committee's aim 'to promote the general powers of the mind', by which they meant, I think, the capacity to construct in the mind an ordered universe of thought and to use fruitfully what Jerome Bruner calls the amplifiers by which mankind has obtained an intellectual grasp of his environment. 'Intellect', said Noel Annan in his Dimbleby lecture, '*that* is what universities exist for. Everything else is secondary.' I suppose the pithiest statement of this aim is E.M. Forster's famous aphorism: 'Only connect.'

If Plato was one of the greatest avatars of this reflective view of life its patron-saint among philosophers was, I suppose, Descartes. It was he who, stimulated by the heat of a large Dutch stove – at what William Temple was tempted to describe as the most disastrous moment in the history of Europe – generated the thesis, immortalized in the tag '*Cogito, ergo sum*', that reflection and contemplation represent the highest expression of human life.

How this aim is best achieved also remains unresolved. My quotations seemed to suggest that breadth of intellectual perspective and grasp was the definitive characteristic of an educated person, but with the galloping increase in the world's stock of knowledge and the constant need to refine and replenish it a narrower but more practicable aim has supervened. This is the study in depth, by scholarship or research, of a specialized branch of knowledge or discipline through which the learner is helped to master its characteristic concepts, its logical structure, the tests of truth it requires and the techniques by which it explores experience. The sanctuary of truth gives way to the sanctuary of intellectual method, with the result that the ideals of general and specialized knowledge uncomfortably rub shoulders. But whether it is knowledge in breadth or knowledge in depth that is in question, it is well identified in my catalogue of aims by Newman's word **Comprehension**.

A third aim springs from a widely different view about the nature of man and the place of knowledge in the educational scheme of things. It has seen the definitive characteristic of *homo sapiens* as being his capacity to form purposes, to weigh alternative courses of action, to reach wise decisions and to act upon them. In this process thought or reflection is to be regarded not as an end in itself but as an inseparable component of rational action. Action indeed has been defined – to distinguish it from physical event or organic behaviour – as human activity guided by knowledge.

In this context, then, the aim of the educator – as opposed to the scholar or researcher – is to help his learners to apply knowledge. For him education is, as Whitehead put it, the acquisition of the art of the utilization of knowledge. 'Pedants', he reminds us, 'sneer at an education which is useful. But if education is not useful what is it? Is it a talent, to be hidden away in a napkin? Of course education should be useful, whatever your aim in life. It was useful to St. Augustine and it was useful to Napoleon.'

Whether it is of general or specialized knowledge that the application and use are in question, our language lacks the vocabulary readily to describe the attributes which those who would emphasize the importance of this aim would like to see developed. The words 'skill' and 'technique' are limited by their respective connotations of physical manipulation and mechanical aptitude. The attempt to fill out their meaning by prefixing the word vocational or occupational fails because, thanks to the unacceptable elitist face of our cultural heritage, these words have suffered parallel debasement. The Greeks had a word for the attributes I am trying to indicate – τεχναι – which in its original meaning conveyed just what I am trying to express. A Greek was described as πολυτεχνησ when he had become skilled in the diverse arts of living. For him, επι τεχνητμαθειν τι meant to learn something personally and professionally in such a manner that body and mind, practice and theory, action and reflection, art and science, emotion and intellect were indissolubly united, with the emphasis on the first term in each pair. The power to harness specialized knowledge to the solution of the practical problems of life, whether personal, professional or social, may conveniently be labelled **Competence**.

It may be the prejudice of an administrator, but there seems to me still to be a vital attribute whose development ranks too low among the educator's major aims. I am thinking of a person's general capacity to manage his own life, to cope with his environment, to profit from experience, to master what used to be called the art of living, to reach sensible decisions and act on them. To call this quality 'gumption' or 'nous' is to incur the charge of vulgarity; to call it 'wisdom' verges on the high-faluting; to call it 'lifemanship' lacks seriousness. May I settle for **Capability** as the nearest I can get to describing the ability to apply one's general stock of knowledge and manifold of skills, as Bacon put it, for the benefit and use of men?

You may well suppose that with cultivation, comprehension, competence and capability the profile of an educated man or woman is now complete. I think not. It is true that in the measure that a person learns these capacities he will be enabled to come to terms with, value, understand and control his environment. But *homo sapiens* is also *homo faber*, a maker, and *homo ludens*, a player. We tend, thanks to the great succession of prophets stretching from Rousseau, through Pestalozzi and Froebel and the sisters MacMillan to Dewey to Piaget, to think of making and playing in terms mainly of the education of young children. But the need for the release of human talent and the liberation of the special gifts that enable each person to contribute something literally unique to the richness of life does not cease to operate at the age of seven, fourteen or even eighteen. There is room in post-eighteen, including higher, education for greater use of the insights that have revolutionized the education of the very young. Many if not most of us may take a modest view of any original contribution that we can make, for example, as designers, artists or musicians, to the quality of life. But it is part of the faith of every good teacher that in every human being there lies hidden, if not the genius of a Michelangelo or a Mozart, at least some nascent bud of originality waiting for the nourishment that will make it blossom. Let me then add **Creativity** to my list of aims. My use of this word does not imply any theory about the extent to which, if at all, it is a potentiality of artists rather than scientists, of divergers rather than convergers, or vice versa. It is just that any battery of educational aims will be defective if it does not allow for the freest possible play to man's originative propensities and imaginative powers.

One final aim seems to me of sovereign importance, difficult though it is to define. A man may be widely and highly cultivated, perfectly comprehending, enviably competent, broadly capable, markedly creative – but at the same time distressingly egocentric. The last and paramount mark of an educated man is surely his capacity to live peaceably and constructively on terms of equality and fellowship with his neighbour. Looked at from the outside this might be described as a capacity for co-operation; felt subjectively it is better represented by such words as conscience, responsibility or obligation. If you have ever been illumined by Jacques Maritain's insistence on the worth of the human person: if you have ever been moved by Albert Schweitzer's dedication to 'reverence for life'; if you have ever been inspired by Martin Buber's invocation of 'the meeting of man with man' in his prose poem *I and Thou*; if, with John Macmurray, you see the function of religion as being to create, maintain and deepen the community of persons and see all education as having in this sense a religious dimension – then you may prefer to call the quality I am trying to feel after by the name of **Communion.** It is the cement that binds together persons-in-community.

I can think of no educational institution, whether nursery, primary, comprehensive or public school, polytechnic or university, college or evening institute through whose curriculum and way of life some trace of each of these aims is not expressed.

While I believe none of them to be dispensable, at all stages of the educational odyssey, and not least in higher education, I should like to see a substantial shift in the centre of gravity from the passive absorption of culture to the active development of creativity and communion; and from mastery of specialized or general knowledge concepts to their translation into what I called competence and capability. That is to say I share Macmurray's happily expressed belief that 'all meaningful knowledge is for the sake of action and all meaningful action is for the sake of friendship.'

If these aims are accepted, the question is: how are they to be realized? Broadly, it is for society, speaking through its many representative voices, somehow to determine through the public discussion of educational aims what kind of people it wants its citizens to become; that it must rest with *the individual learner* to decide what capacities or qualities he stands in need of developing; and that it is for teachers and academics, in the autonomous exercise of their professional skills, to help him clarify and realize his aims. In other words, however powerful the attractive pull of the educational goals set before the learner his success in achieving them will depend on the strength and direction of the motives and needs that propel him. It is possible to identify at least some of these.

There are those who rejoice in the challenge of physical effort or constructive skill who want simply to improve their performance and to prove to their own satisfaction that, in the teeth of Browning, a man's grasp may exceed his reach. Call this motive pride.

Then there are those who, in the biblical phrase, have come to themselves and want to make good the absence or misuse of earlier chances. This motive has helped to inspire such varied responses as compensatory and literacy programmes, the extra-mural movement, the Open University and the student-shaped Dip.HE courses pioneered by the School of Independent Studies of the North-East London Polytechnic. Call this motive retrieval.

There are those with time on their hands – thanks perhaps to retirement, temporary redundancy or, alas, unemployment – who want to use it more fruitfully or enjoyably: they need what might be called life-enhancing occupation.

The great majority, at the point of leaving school at eighteen or earlier, and tens of thousands at later stages in their lives simply want to qualify for a good job or range of jobs. The results of every opinion survey I have seen reinforce the commonsense view that this is the most powerful and widespread motive for immediate or deferred post-eighteen education. It is time we ceased to disparage it. Let us forswear the sanctimonious humbug by which (contrary to our own practice as parents) we judge the educational value of courses by the negative criterion that they are non-vocational. If research and scholarship are not vocations, nothing is. Neither in this respect nor in their call for specialist preparation do they differ from gas-fitting, hairdressing, business management, pharmacy or teaching. In the modern world, then, the need for training constitutes an almost universal motive.

Then there are those who look to post-eighteen education to improve, not so much their occupational chances, as their general capacity to cope with the varied roles of *homo sociologicus*. They want to become, for example, better marriage partners, better parents, better playgroup organizers, better public speakers, better negotiators. They want to practise these skills under expert guidance – an urge for rehearsal.

There are others again who, while they set their sights far short of high academic achievement, wish to measure themselves against some standard, to reach a goal they have set themselves, as modest perhaps as 'O' or 'A' level. They are actuated by, in the best sense of the word, ambition.

Distinguishable from the motives I have mentioned and somewhat at a discount is people's felt need to become better members of the community, to improve their social and political understanding and competence: a quest for better citizenship.

While the next motive may seem to be linked more closely with medicine than education, I know of many people who seek education to defeat loneliness or overcome the loss of personal confidence: members, for example, of one-parent families marooned on huge impersonal housing estates. Their need is therapy.

Akin to them are the growing number of people who feel their world is falling apart, who cannot withstand without help the impact on their lives of the accelerating thrust of change. They feel at sea. They look to education to re-set their compasses, to give them new bearings – victims of what Alvin Toffler called 'Future Shock'. They seek, in a word, orientation.

The explosion of knowledge has given all those whose work is grounded in their diminishing stock of specialized knowledge a new incentive constantly to replenish it. One of the mainsprings of lifelong education goes then by the old-fashioned name of 'renewal'.

Lastly, there is the motive that most teachers would like to see as the dominant one in their clients: intellectual curiosity, the urge to understand the nature and meanings of things. Let me call it, simply, 'search'.

These somewhat arbitrarily selected motives have not been, and should not be arranged in any order of merit: not, for example, by reference to the amount, difficulty, purity or prestige of the knowledge or to the current social valuation of the skills that their satisfaction entails. It is just as important to the barber as it is to the surgeon (perhaps more?) to further his own education, however each conceives of that process. My own belief is that these motives deserve our equal respect and sympathy.

# CHAPTER 6
# New Ways to Learn
*Tyrrell Burgess*

So far this book has been about the damaging imbalance in British education and the ways in which it might be corrected. In this chapter I wish to propose a basis for an educational solution. What we need, and what I hope to describe, are new ways to learn.

The strength of the dominant tradition in education rests upon assumptions about knowledge, learning and education which are accepted without question throughout education and society. The prestige of our universities and sixth forms derives from the convention that they know what they are doing. It seems only the plainest common sense that those who have spent a lifetime in the study of a subject, who have become specialist and expert in it, should be those who can say not only what the subject is and what are its characteristic insights and techniques, but can also introduce to its mysteries the less educated and less expert. There is a phrase used by academics which is in my experience unquestioned as a statement of what they do – that is, 'the preservation, extension and dissemination of knowledge'. If one talks to teachers of vocational skills one finds that their expressions are different, but their purpose is the same. And for all the accompanying claims about developing the individual which are uttered by teachers in both schools and colleges, it is clear that they mostly expect to do so through instruction in various branches of knowledge. If this view of knowledge is right, we are condemned, I believe, to the dominance of tradition and we must reconcile ourselves to the permanence of our frustration and criticism of education.

Fortunately we do not have to accept this view of knowledge at all. The dominant tradition in education, so far from being soundly based, rests in my view on assumptions about knowledge which are quite simply mistaken and on grounds which are intellectually and practically worthless.

It may be thought that the claim that our universities, colleges and schools rest on intellectually worthless foundations is a bold claim to make. Let us approach the matter more gently by looking first into the activities of teaching and learning. What is done in educational institutions is not only consistent from place to place all over the world, but has been so, I am told, since Aristotle. Young people in formal education attend lectures, seminars or tutorials. They read books, write essays for their teachers' judgement, watch demonstrations. They may carry out 'experiments'; that is, they go through prescribed procedures in order to see for themselves some established process at work. They may get to do project work. In relatively rich places, the students may get a lot of individual attention: elsewhere they are dealt with very much in groups. In large institutions there may be a wide choice of subjects and of teachers; in smaller places there may be no choice at all. Usually, but not always, the higher the level, the more independence the student may have. Usually, though unnecessarily, arts students have more independence than science students. Throughout, the object of all these activities is to cover a set amount of knowledge (the course, curriculum, syllabus) and then convince the examiners that one has done so.

These are the externals of education, the name we give to the events we arrange. But what is happening? What takes place when the student learns and when the teacher teaches? I confess that when I first came to consider this I was shocked at how little was known. For example, most of the current theories are based upon the learning habits of those pigeons, rats and circus apes that have had the misfortune to be captured by learning theorists. The theories are many, and they conflict. But whatever the differences between these theories, they all have one characteristic in common. They hold that learning takes place through the activity of the learner. Traditional practice, however, implicity assumes that learning takes place through the activity of the teacher. Teachers have and control subjects, disciplines and bodies of knowledge, and the taught do not. Teachers present their material and the taught acquire and then reproduce it. Unfortunately this almost universal practice among teachers flies in the face of what is almost universally agreed about learning. Teaching and learning are, in our current practice, largely disconnected. Indeed, there appear to be two kinds of need in the world: the need to learn and the need to teach. These two needs are at war: the one is incompatible with the other. In other words, the failure of our educational institutions is at heart an educational failure. It is because they fail in education that they are so disappointing to individuals and to society.

This conclusion requires some explanation. To put it mildly, school and college teachers are not, on the whole, stupid. Nor do people go into teaching because they are filled with ill will or loathe their fellow men. Teachers do what they do because they believe it to be right, and many of them show great humanity and ingenuity in mitigating in practice the worst effects of their implicit theories and beliefs.

Why is it then that teachers think it right – indeed, accept without question – to act in ways that neglect or even oppose what they know about learning? The answer, I think, is partly that theories of learning are unsatisfactory and unconvincing (and are incompatible with each other), and partly that teachers, like most people, have an implicit view of knowledge on which their practice depends but which chimes ill with theories of learning. What we need, in short, is a theory which better explains how people learn and which is consistent with a theory of knowledge.

Most people have what one might describe as an accumulative view of knowledge. It seems obvious that more is known now than was known 100 years ago. Over the centuries bodies of knowledge have been built up through the accumulation of facts. In recent centuries men have come to believe that a particular kind of knowledge, scientific knowledge, is an especially secure and reliable kind. It began with the physical sciences, but other sciences have aspired to the same kind of security. It was and is believed that what gives scientific knowledge its characteristic quality and security is its method. On this view, scientists base their activity upon observation – carefully controlled and measured observation. They record their findings, publish them and accumulate data. From this they may formulate hypotheses which fit the facts and explain the causal relations between them. They then seek evidence to support the hypothesis, and if the latter is thus verified they have established another law or theory.

Science, on this view, is the accumulation of certainties based on observation and experimental evidence: numberless observations lead to a hypothesis which when verified is established as a law. This method of basing laws on accumulated observations is known as induction, and has for centuries been seen as the hallmark of science.

Of course the idea of induction has itself caused problems. It was David Hume who first spotted the logical difficulty which gave philosophers a good deal of trouble. The difficulty is that numberless confirming observations cannot give us any assurance that the next observation will be the same. Bertrand Russell in particular was worried that the rationality of science depended on a principle – induction – which could not itself be rationally defended.

The boldest solution to the problem of induction has been offered by Karl Popper, who says bluntly, '. . . there is no induction, because universal theories are not deducible from singular statements. But they may be refuted by singular statements, since they may clash with descriptions of observable facts.'[1] For Popper the logic of scientific discovery is as follows: scientific discussions, he says, start with a problem $(P_1)$, to which we offer a tentative theory (TT) or solution, hypothesis or conjecture. The theory is then criticized, to try to eliminate error (EE) – whereupon the theory and its critical revision give rise to new problems $(P_2)$. As Popper puts it, 'science begins with problems and ends with problems.' But it does not begin and end with the same problems: $P_2$ is always different from $P_1$ – which is why we can speak of scientific progress. Popper sets this theory out as a schema or formula the importance of which has been overlooked by people who feel that if something is clear it must be trivial. This is it: $P_1{\rightarrow}TT{\rightarrow}EE{\rightarrow}P_2$.

Each step in this formulation, and its place in the sequence, has important consequences. It asserts, for example, the primacy of problems. The beginning of an inquiry is *not* the attempt to solve a problem (the tentative theory comes second, not first): it is the problem itself, and it is important to work as hard as possible on the formulation of problems before searching for solutions. This is because success in the latter often depends upon success in the former. An enormous amount of time and energy is wasted in the world by people who jump straight into solutions, and concentrate upon the difficulties of these – without pausing to consider whether they are apt for the problem formulated or even without formulating a problem at all. It is also misleading to talk of 'identifying' problems, as if the problems were sitting there waiting for us. They are not. Problem-formulation is a creative activity.

Nor should one be misled by the word 'tentative'. A theory is tentative because it has to be tested: it does not have to be half-hearted. Indeed, the bolder and more definite it is the better it can be tested. What we need are theories with a high informative content, because the more information they contain the more likely they are to be false, but if they survive our best efforts to falsify them, they have enabled us to make a correspondingly large progress in understanding. The best theories are the most daring leaps of imagination, and science, like art, is an expression of the human spirit.

Error elimination is the process of expressing our theories in ways which can be tested. And the object of the test is to falsify the theory. This step is nearly as often neglected as the first – or is widely misunderstood. Neglect resides in the uncritical acceptance of theories, and in the unwillingness to consider what would falsify them. Misunderstanding arises because people think that the object of tests (or experiments) is to confirm a theory. But no amount of confirmation can make a theory more secure, and our knowledge remains as it was. But one falsification can destroy a theory, and our knowledge advances. We are ready to formulate the new problems.

With the introduction of falsifiability we reach Popper's criterion which demarcates science from non-science. This is itself one of those bold leaps of imagination whose consequences are only now being slowly realized. For example, it means that all knowledge, including scientific knowledge, is provisional, and always will be. We cannot prove that what we know is true, and it may turn out to be false. The best we can do is to justify our preference for one theory rather than another. Disciplines, even scientific disciplines are not bodies of established fact: they are changing all the time, and not by the accumulation of new certainties. Of course, we assume the truth of our existing knowledge for practical purposes and are quite right to do so; but we must be ready for it to be superseded. What Popper has done is to replace the notion of certainty in science, and in all human knowledge, with the idea of progress. We cannot be sure that we have the truth: we can, however, systematically eliminate error. The way we eliminate error is by testing. In particular, observations are not used as the basis of a theory, but are derived from a theory and are used to test it. He says 'that observations, and even more so observation statements and statements of experimental results, are always *interpretations* of the facts observed; that they are *interpretations in the light of theories.*'[2]

What is interesting about Popper's theory of knowledge is that it is consistent with his theory of learning: indeed, it is the same theory. Learning of any kind, not just discovery at the frontiers of knowledge, takes place through the formulation of problems and through trial and error in solving these problems.

There have been many eminent scientists who have testified to the insight which Popper's theory gives them into their own scientific activity. I want to claim that it offers an equal insight to educators. In particular it should persuade us to question the basis of what we do. It appears to me that the organization and practice of modern education, both academically and institutionally, rests upon an implicit acceptance of induction; in other words upon a fallacy. It is impossible to speak, as academics do, of the preservation, extension and dissemination of knowledge unless one has in mind the gradual accumulation of certainties. The whole idea of the preservation of knowledge is alien to scientific method: what we should be seeking to do is destroy our present theories. The organization of subject departments is defensible if they are small groups working on the problems of the subject, but not if they are (as they are) bureaucracies for the issue of established bodies of fact.

It is accepted that one needs to have a first degree before one can do research: as if to say to the students, 'When you know enough you can start to think.' The whole activity of teaching, in lectures, seminars, tutorials or what you will, is explicable only on the basis that knowledge exists and can be imparted. The presence of courses, syllabuses and curricula assumes that knowledge is independent of problems. Few people ever ask, 'To what problem is this degree course a solution?' If they do, the answer is seldom other than the problem of getting a degree. The examinations at the end of these courses test little more than the accumulation and manipulation of knowledge. The problems they pose are seldom more serious than the problem of passing the examination. Nor does the ideal of a community of scholars survive in practice the division between the teachers and the taught: the one with the duty to know and impart, the other with the duty to accept and to learn.

Of course, there have been many people with this sense of unease about the practice of education. More important, there have been many teachers who have either instinctively, or after worrying thought, tried to organize learning rather than teaching. They have encouraged 'discovery methods', project work and independent learning. But they have been under attack, partly because these methods still sit uneasily in the rest of the system (how, for instance, does one examine such work?), and partly because they have been unable to give as coherent an intellectual account of themselves as is claimed by traditional academics. This insecurity is no longer justified. It is the traditional academic practice which needs to be defended.

What we have, in fact, is a continuum of learning, whose logic is the same, from the new-born babe to the research worker on the frontiers of knowledge. Each is engaged in the formulation of problems, in solving them and in testing the solutions. Most people will formulate problems that have been formulated many times before. Their proposed solutions will be familiar; their tests commonplace. But they will *learn* by this activity. They will not learn better or faster if we parcel up received solutions to problems formulated by others: indeed this is an anti-learning process. Moreover, it inhibits the possibility of progress, because it is always possible that someone will formulate a common problem differently, will propose a different solution or a more effective test.

At the other end of the continuum are those people engaged on formulating problems which have remained unformulated in the past, and who are leading the attack upon ignorance at its strongest. They may indeed be working in a discipline, upon the problems of the discipline, though it is a commonplace of scientific discovery that the successful formulation of problems may involve breaking through the limits of a discipline. The leap of imagination required of them may be enormous, but the nature of their activity is not arcane. We are all learners: in logic we are equals. I hope I have said enough to convince you why it is that education remains disappointing, and why it will continue to disappoint unless we can make an assault on the presuppositions which underlie it, and the content of courses and syllabuses which grow from these assumptions. If education is to offer any help towards solving the problems of individuals or of society, it must do so directly by helping individuals to formulate problems and to propose and test solutions. It cannot do so by its present practice of offering (in Popper's striking phrase) 'unwanted answers to unasked questions'.

There is something more to be said about problems and their formulation, if only because in my experience the idea of problems gives people trouble. In Popper's formulation of the logic of discovery he uses, interchangeably and often all together, a number of words for the second term of his schema – theory, solution, hypothesis, conjecture. This practice presumably derives from his impatience with discussions of meaning, which he regards as trivial. He does not wish understanding to be limited by definitions. What is more, it is part of what he is arguing that theories are solutions to problems, and solutions, even to practical problems, are theories. What is more, it is important to remember that the *logic* of the process is the same whatever the problems which are being tackled and at whatever level. I believe, however, that it is important to distinguish different kinds of problems. Indeed, a failure to make this distinction vitiates much of our social as well as our educational practice. Let me give some examples. There are problems of what is the case, which we can call scientific problems. There are problems of how to get from one state of affairs to another, which we can call engineering problems (to use the examples of one engineer: how to get from one side of a river to another, or from bread to toast). There are formal problems: those of mathematics, for example, or chess. There are philosophical problems, which include ethical and aesthetic problems.

Most people are concerned with the second of these kinds of problems: the engineering or practical problems. They need to know how to get from one state of affairs to another. Their problems concern their homes, families, jobs, incomes and leisure. They typically want to change their circumstances. In this they often believe that education will be a help.

Unfortunately they find that educators are preoccupied with the other kinds of problems and will fill them up with ready-made scientific, formal and philosophical solutions. The courses offered presuppose that a grasp of these solutions must precede the tackling of practical problems. There was a very instructive moment in the first programme of Bryan Magee's brilliant television series on philosophy[3] when Sir Isaiah Berlin tried to say what philosophical problems were. He identified three of my four kinds of problems – ignoring entirely the practical or engineering kind. On the other hand, his example of a philosophical problem was one which grew directly from a practical one (it concerned the ethical question of whether an interrogator should lie in order to extract information from a prisoner). It is clear that Sir Isaiah's educational practice was at war with his theories. In seeking to make things clear he used a practical problem, but he did not think practical problems worthy of inclusion in his list of different kinds of problems. I believe most people come to scientific and formal problems, as well as philosophical ones, through their concern with practical or engineering problems. They come to be interested in these other kinds of problems through their desire to solve practical ones. And they learn in the areas of these other kinds of problems so much the better if they come to them through trying to solve a practical problem which concerns them deeply. But they find academics uninterested in this.

Let me give another example of what I mean. In order to be an engineer in England you have to be certified as such, after a period of practice, by one of the engineering institutions. In order to qualify for such a certificate you have to take an engineering degree in a university or polytechnic. In order to do that degree you usually have to have studied physics at 'A' level. In order to study physics at 'A' level you have to have studied mathematics at 'O' level. I do not regard this as a plausible way of producing a decent engineer or of teaching anybody mathematics or physics. It would be preferable, in my view, if aspiring engineers were faced directly with the problems of engineering. They would find no difficulty in recognizing the value of the mathematics and physics they needed and would have the incentive, denied them by the other method, of learning it.

What then, are the consequences of the logic of learning and of discovery for the practice of education? I believe them to be shattering. In the first place, what is important is not a particular fact or even a particular ordered collection of facts, but *method*. It is method rather than information which gives mastery, and it is method which must be the chief business of education. Nor is there any need to insist upon a particular field of human interest in which scientific method can be understood: an educator can use any interest of the student as a vehicle.

Second, it is clear that existing subject disciplines are ways of organizing knowledge from particular points of view. They were so organized to solve the problems of their practitioners. But these problems may no longer actually be those even of existing practitioners, let alone those of students and potential students. The presentation of knowledge as bodies of organized facts is a way of ensuring its unhelpfulness to most people.

Third, the provisional nature of knowledge suggests caution in regarding education as involving the accumulation of it. This is recognized increasingly as educators and their students find that it is possible, indeed normal, for the knowledge painfully acquired to become quickly out of date. Unfortunately the educators' solution is to offer 'refresher' or 'up-dating' courses, so that the students can have their obsolete knowledge replaced by some more, which will itself become obsolete in turn. There can be no sense in this process.

Fourth, since criticism is of the essence of the method, education must offer opportunities for students to be critical and to use criticism. It cannot, even (indeed especially) for the sake of instruction, ask the students to accept the greater knowledge, experience, and wisdom of the teacher.

This implies, fifth, that it is the students who must take the initiative in planning their own education. There can be little justification for the prior imposition of curricula and syllabuses. Such curricula must necessarily presuppose purposes which may not be the students'.

Sixth, in testing the efficacy of the education provided we shall need to examine what it is the student can *do*, rather than what he knows. The latter always was a somewhat arbitrary proceeding, since even if the most successful undergraduate were to know all that an undergraduate *could* know, his knowledge would still be infinitesimal. Since we can know so little (and since what we know is provisional) we can at least learn how to do something – and what we can most sensibly do is tackle our own problems.

Most important, perhaps, this view of education cannot exclude people, on the ground that they do not know enough, or have not had so many years' previous education, or do not show an aptitude for a subject. These educational arrogances have a place only in a superseded view of knowledge.

We are, in short, face to face with the chance of a creative revolution in education, by accepting the logic of learning: by organizing education at all levels explicitly round the formulation of problems, the proposal of solutions and the testing of these solutions.

## References

1  POPPER, K.R. (1976). Unended Quest: *An Intellectual Autobiography*. London: Fontana.
2  POPPER, K.R. (1959). *The Logic of Scientific Discovery*. London: Hutchinson.
3  MAGEE, B. (1978). *Man of Ideas*. London: BBC.

# CHAPTER 7
# The Outcomes of Education

*Elizabeth Adams*

In Britain today there is widespread concern about the outcomes
of education, but little agreement as to how to improve matters.
This chapter begins by considering some of the inadequacies still
found in a system which, for forty years, has been legally required
to provide primary and secondary education for all according to
age, ability and aptitude.

Next, it will indicate some recent responses to the problem of
dissatisfaction with the outcomes, particularly of secondary
education. Examples are given of responses both by those directly
involved in the system, and by other members of society seeking
value for the national investment in public education. Finally, a
proposal will be outlined as to what could be done to encourage
and accredit the acquisition of competence and of personal
capability. The proposed solution is compatible with the present
distribution of powers and duties between the central and local
authorities, the school governors, teachers, parents and students.

## Inadequacies

The legal position concerning compulsory education is that it must
be provided for young people according to age, ability and
aptitude. Apart from certain requirements concerning religious
instruction, the law makes no curricular demands. Nor are any
formal assessments called for. It would seem, therefore, that since
1944 there have been several decades of opportunity to work
towards the fulfilment of whatever educational aims society and
the professionals identified. One might have hoped that as time

passed, the outcomes of education would become increasingly satisfactory. Unfortunately, however, there is much evidence to the contrary: evidence of inadequacies in the system and of widespread dissatisfaction with its products. What has gone wrong?

One cannot blame the authors of the Education Act of 1944 for the present malaise. Rather, one must criticize for lack of vision those empowered to implement the Act. Many of them do not appear to have tried to ensure that each boy and girl developed as fully as possible. Often, they seem to have failed to appreciate that the nation's well-being depends on its human resources. In the early days many administrators allowed post-war shortages of buildings and of graduate teachers to justify retaining various familiar features of the pre-war pattern of education. For example, to replace the old scholarship system, selection at eleven-plus was made near-universal. This determined whether a primary pupil was transferred to a former secondary school, renamed 'grammar', or to a former senior elementary school, renamed 'secondary modern'. The eleven-plus procedures accustomed people to the idea that unless a young person was successful at this first hurdle, he was ineligible for consideration for later stages of academic competition (unless, of course, his parents had the will and the means to opt for an independent school). For school students the next hurdle was, and remains, public examinations at sixteen-plus.[1]

As the years passed, the influence of the eleven-plus was eroded and a more complicated system of sixteen-plus examinations became available to all.[2] However, the outcomes of secondary education continued to be reckoned in terms only of sixteen-plus examination results. The position throughout the present century and still obtaining is that those who leave school before reaching the age at which a public examination can be taken, or whose teachers are not prepared to recommend them as examination candidates, have nothing to show for their years of compulsory education. Nobody is in any position to judge whether their time has been spent suitably according to their age, ability and aptitude. They may have acquired different skills, and they may possess varied qualities of importance to their outlook and prospects in life. Their teachers may have helped them develop good characteristics. But as students and teachers are given no 'credit' for non-measurable attributes, their acquisition tends not to be planned, resourced or formally recorded.

**Responses**

In recent years, dissatisfaction with the inadequacies of school education has been voiced by individuals, pressure groups and politicians, on radio and television and in books, journals and newspapers. That so many people from a wide range of walks of life saw fit to sign the Education for Capability Manifesto of the Royal Society of Arts is, in itself, evidence of widespread recognition of the inadequacies of the outcomes of education. In response to this growing criticism, positive action is beginning to change the face of education without altering its structure. Many secondary schools have made great curricula changes individually and have joined with others in such groups as the Centre for the Study of Curriculum in Secondary Schools (CSCS) to share experience and plan progress.[3] A number of local education authorities have produced guidelines for development, such as the consultative document published by Coventry Education Committee, *Comprehensive Education for Life*.[4] Others, such as Oxfordshire, have consulted with a university examinations board to modify the effects of sixteen-plus examinations: while a nationwide effort involving all secondary schools has been made to produce for these subject examinations joint criteria which will be acceptable to the Secretary of State for Education.

Many responses to the present inadequacies of the educational system have developed because a rapidly declining national economy is causing concern to everybody. The educational system is taking some of the blame for the failure to sustain levels of employment and industrial competitiveness. Curiously, however, official responses have largely focused on the post-compulsory stage, seeking to remedy the effects of inadequate schooling rather than to come to grips with its causes. Government efforts have been directed more towards ameliorating the employment situation for young people than towards facilitating enlightened educational practices in school.

In 1977 the Secretary of State for Employment asked the Manpower Services Commission to set up a new programme of opportunities for unemployed young people aged sixteen to eighteen. The ensuing Youth Opportunities Programme began the following year and generated a new language of acronyms such as WEEP (Work Experience on Employers' Premises). This language, however, did not reach all schools as the Manpower Services Commission communicated with local education authorities mainly through the Careers Service. Few schools will have seen *Making Experience Work*[5] published by the Special Service Programmes Division of the Manpower Services Commission to provide principles and guidelines. Still less were schools likely to have been influenced by the publications of the Further Education Unit which produced, in 1979, *A Basis for Choice*,[6] a seminal document now referred to as the ABC.

The ABC was a report of a study group on post-sixteen pre-employment courses. It listed a dozen aims of the common core of curriculum without once referring to the subjects which mainly constitute school curricula. Instead, it said that the curriculum should bring about a basis for making informed and realistic decisions regarding the future; an ability to develop satisfactory personal relationships; competence in a variety of study skills; a capacity to plan and evaluate courses of action; a development of everyday coping skills; and a flexibility of attitude and willingness to learn.

Whatever the impact of these publications, the deepening economic recession had the effect of stimulating action. The Manpower Services Commission published *A New Training Initiative* in 1981,[7] which was followed by a White Paper, *NTI, a Programme for Action*.[8] The consultative document claimed to offer to the education service a realization of many hopes and aspirations for young people and a key role, in partnership with employers and unions, in positive action, at the same time *requiring* that some traditional approaches and values be modified or abandoned.

In the following year, 1982, the Manpower Services Commission and the Further Education Unit issued a joint statement of agreement on curricular design and implementation.[9] This brief statement clarified some of the emerging principles concerning the training and education of young people which were common to the Manpower Services Commission, the Further Education Unit and the White Paper. For example, the document of progress mentioned in the White Paper, the portfolio of assessment described by the Manpower Services, and the Further Education Unit's student profile were seen to be all basically the same thing. There was agreement also that all should have in common the ability 'to show what an individual can do and not where he has failed.'

At the same time as these statements were being made, various researches conducted on behalf of the Manpower Services Commission were beginning to report. The Department of Psychology in the University of Sheffield worked on the grouping of skills with the specific objective of developing and standardizing a method for assessing the skill requirements of young people's jobs. They made a Job Components Inventory and tested it out with three local education authorities.[10] Other studies of occupational 'clusters' or 'families' were carried out by the Institute of Manpower Studies and published as a report: *Foundation Training Issues.*[11]

The responses from national bodies mentioned so far in this chapter have not sought to remedy the main problem bedevilling the secondary schools: that of how to make examinations subserve curricula. Had this issue been dealt with years ago, as was intended, the present crisis of confidence in the outcomes of compulsory education might have been averted. The fact is not generally appreciated that two unequal bodies were joined twenty years ago to form the national Schools Council for Curriculum and Examinations to achieve just that purpose.[12] The task was daunting and the battle was never joined. The opportunity was thrown away. From the outset, the long-established Secondary Schools Examination Council pulled rank over the recently-formed Curriculum Study Group and the ascendency of examination interests went unchallenged. It may be that the task would have proved impossible. The position now, however, is that the Schools Council has been disbanded. The two elements are more unequal than ever with the new Secondary Examinations Council responsible for advising the Secretary of State as a matter of urgency concerning the new joint sixteen-plus examination proposals.

This story only underlines the point that the real issue for education in our country is the accreditation of its outcomes. Despite a great national investment in curriculum development the position at present remains as it has been for many years: credit is given for providing evidence under examination conditions of familiarity with certain bodies of knowledge pre-determined in the syllabuses of the examination boards. This fact conditions students and teachers to devote school time to examinable content and to consider other uses of educational opportunities as a waste. Many teachers are keen to develop experimental curricula of the kind produced during the heyday of the Schools Council, but are inhibited from doing so by genuine fear of lessening their students' chances in their examinations.[13]

The penetration early in 1983 of the secondary stage of education by the Manpower Services Commission is the only national experiment, to date, touching the crisis in the schools themselves.[14] The response of schools and local education authorities to the chance of funding for innovative projects gives some measure of the schools' need to legitimate enterprise. It demonstrates that students, teachers and employers are bored with subject-based school curricula dictated by examination syllabuses. So far, however, few people seem to be taking the Manpower Services Commission's intervention seriously. The group of businessmen and educators who came together during 1983 to plan *Education 2000*[15] did not include any representative. Nor, of course, was the Department of Employment, of which the Manpower Services is a part, mentioned in the *Policy Statement*[16] of the Department of Education on the work of Her Majesty's Inspectorate.

**Proposal**

Manpower Services Commission activities, however, as well as public examinations and other assessments used in school could all be accommodated in the author's proposal for dealing with the problem of the accreditation of the outcomes of education. The proposal, first mooted in 1980,[17] is to create a framework within which national recognition is given to what each individual school does for its students. The proposal, in brief, is for the programmes of study for students aged fourteen to sixteen to be validated by an external body; and for the ultimate school Statement describing each sixteen year-old to be accredited by a different, more prestigious external body, linked to a national headquarters office responsible for policy decisions conerning accreditation of the outcomes of compulsory education to the Department of Education and Science. This general pattern is adapted from the success of the School for Independent Study at the North East London Polytechnic (see p.146) in gaining accreditation by the Council for National Academic Awards for individual programmes of study.[18] Given the support of the external Validating Board these programmes replace the syllabus, which is what is normally accredited. Students have much involvement in decisions regarding their use of their time at college and, if successful, leave with a Dip.HE or, after three years, an Honours degree: and often also with a clear view of their own potential and of the career possibilities open to them.

In proposing a framework on these lines for secondary schools the aim is to ensure that every young person completes compulsory education with something substantial to show for his or her years at school. During the two years before the age of sixteen each student would build up a folder of evidence of his work for his own retention and to serve as a basis for an agreed school statement summarizing his capacities, achievements, interests and ambitions. This process would help parents, teachers and future employers by encouraging young people to commit themselves to school work and to higher standards of achievement.

Although schools vary (for example there are eleven to sixteen schools and fourteen to eighteen schools) most young people are asked to choose 'options' at the end of the year in which they reach the age of thirteen; that is, when they have still two full years of compulsory education ahead. It is proposed that at this options stage there should be a planning period giving young people time to think through and discuss with teachers and parents how they think their next two years of school should be spent. They should help to set out a two-year educational programme likely to help them solve their personal, academic, vocational or other problems. In present circumstances, such a programme would include preparation for public examinations and perhaps also for graded tests (in subjects such as music and languages). The acceptance of some responsibility for planning should encourage young people to begin to take charge of their own circumstances so that they reach sixteen not only knowledgeable but competent and independent. For teachers, the planning will call for new skills. They will no longer be required only to teach to a syllabus but to respond directly to what young people themselves need. As John Raven has repeatedly pointed out in research, most teachers want to do this;[19] but so far they have lacked time and incentive, while neither training nor experience has given them much acquaintance with the exercise of accurate empathy.

From the point of view of the student and of his teachers, the essential characteristics of the proposal are to have an opportunity for students to show initiative, to use a formal planning period responsibly, to make a commitment to work and to adapt to different forms of school timetable including tutorial and special interest study periods.

The student will have personal tutorship and be enabled and encouraged to build up a folder of evidence of his capabilities, knowing that it will be taken into account in the final summarizing statement from the school. However, the proposal involves more than the students themselves and their teachers and tutors. The other partners in the preparation of accredited school statements of the outcomes of education for sixteen year-olds are the head of the school and the senior staff; the school governing body; the validating board and the accrediting board. As the last two boards are novel to the school system, these will be described now, to clarify the discussion about the proposal. The proposal makes no recommendations concerning curriculum; and gives no advice about assessments, examinations or profiles. Each school is expected to conduct its affairs with the freedom already available to it and with its accountability to its governors and to the local education authority unchanged.[20] What the proposal does is to outline a framework of accreditation which should enable each school to improve the outcomes of education for its students by enabling credit to be given for more than examination results. It is expected that every secondary school will have a set of agreed notes or a handbook of guidance describing the school's aims and procedures (at least as they affect the fourteen to sixteen age group) and that copies are available to teachers, governors, students and parents, as necessary. The head of the school is responsible for such notes or guidelines and may well have discussed them with the governing body, the local authority advisory service or Her Majesty's Inspectorate. The head will also have made sure that these notes are fully accepted by the teaching staff and are explained to new members of staff and governors.

In many schools, however, it does not appear to be felt necessary to spell out the connection between these aims and the syllabuses of 'O' level and CSE examinations to which much of the work of the fourteen to sixteen year old group is devoted. Many young students are drafted into classes and courses with little idea of the expected content and less about its possible use or interest to them. The grouping may have been made with the greatest skill by their teachers, but the boys and girls made no commitments regarding particular subjects and were simply put into the classes for which they seemed best fitted. Examination courses should not be seen only as a means to an end. Young people have to be helped to make their own choices and to take as much responsibility as they can for the use of their own school time. There are too many bored youngsters in school – including many with high endowments – whose motivation and goodwill towards study are needlessly thrown away.

Apart from examination courses the connection between the school guidelines and the student's needs are often not clear, at least not to the young person. Many boys and girls are not aiming at academic life.[21] They know that varied capabilities will be of practical use to them in their homes, jobs and interests. But in few schools do they have much say in developing these. There are many young people with particular needs which could be catered for if they were seriously considered. The basic skills of spoken and written language often call for a determined effort by all concerned. Children whose mother tongue is not English have special problems with which they need sustained help. Young people with outstanding gifts in music or artistic expression cannot afford to wait until after 'O' level to give much attention to their art. The list is endless. Not later than the age of thirteen or fourteen, young people should make a realistic commitment to the pursuit of the skills and competencies they need and want.

To ensure that no pupil was wasting time on foolish projects and to satisfy the public that the work in progress at any school was suitable to the students, a validation procedure is proposed. Membership of a validating board would have been agreed between the head, the governors and the local authority. One or more members would already be governors. Others might be local business men, academics, advisers. When the thirteen to fourteen year-olds' programmes (their statement of intent) had been prepared and agreed with the staff, a full-day meeting should be held at which these programmes could be 'defended'. The head would act as clerk to the formal meetings of the validating board and would take into consideration every criticism of school study programmes that emerged. Any re-negotiation that seemed urgent would be dealt with subsequently by the head with the member of staff and the students concerned. The school would remain responsible for its planning and timetabling but would benefit from the criticism of the validating board. To the extent to which members of the validating board themselves came to grips with the problem of suiting school courses to the needs of the students, good relations would be built up in the neighbourhood. The goodwill of business firms, local colleges or other institutions would develop through genuine discussion.

Once validated, it would be for the school to cater as well as it could for all the demands from students on staffing and resources. Students should be given timetables designed to meet their needs as far as possible, and should be trained to monitor their own progress by building up their file of evidence. Parents would be invited to help sustain the young people's interest in their growing capabilities and to support their efforts at identifying suitable items as evidence.

During the two years of the programme some students might have to re-negotiate their contracts on account of illness or changes in home circumstances. A few students would arrive at the school, transferred from elsewhere, who would need help in finding their niche. The provision that the school could make might be altered by changes of staff. In general, however, the plan would be to pursue the study programmes as intended and agreed at the outset. The knowledge that planning was 'for real' would soon help to build up among younger pupils expectations about this procedure and would sustain the efforts of older students and staff. Throughout the two years of the programme each school would keep its own records of student progress in whatever way seemed appropriate.

To date, few schools have found elaborate profiling systems to be either practicable or sound[22] but the framework suggested here does not rule out any mode of recording that a school decides is worthwhile. What it does suggest is that evidence of capability, interest and progress is more convincing than a teacher's assessment given in marks, letters or grades. If a student produces high quality embroidery or conjures up a mathematical game, actual evidence of this attainment means more to the student himself or herself, to parents, and to employers than does a mark on a chart. When it comes to assessing personal qualities most teachers are hard put to it to know what to do as the traditional classroom offers limited opportunity for observation. Facts such as punctuality and attendance can be readily noted. They could well be monitored by students themselves.

A great deal of work has gone into attempts at recording student achievement and student characteristics since the studies pioneered in Scotland in the mid-seventies.[23] The Schools Council has published a description of attempts of twenty-one schools to develop records of achievement at sixteen-plus.[24] The City and Guilds of London Institute has conducted several research projects on reporting basic abilities in profile form[25] and on the validity of profiling.[26] A number of local authorities have sponsored profiling projects. No-one is claiming that the problem is solved. Every school is free to do what it thinks best regarding its records and school reports. What is being promulgated here is the co-operation of the student in planning and monitoring his course of study with teachers/tutors who have helped think it through with the individual needs of the student uppermost in mind.

This is a simple idea. What makes it different is the accompanying proposal for accreditation. As a rule, accreditation is given only to courses of study, defined in syllabuses of examinations. Once accepted as a creditable syllabus, the examination is in the hands of examiners appointed by examination boards. Standards of success and failure are determined by experience in marking the papers written by candidates. While great care is taken to make proper judgements, no-one should imagine that standards are other than matters of judgement based on experience. Judgements about grades are not absolute and are not comparable: not between papers in the same subject; nor between papers in different subjects; nor between different years.[27]

Unfortunately, the results of examinations sound convincing and are often used as though they defined people in rank order of general competence. Descriptive statements about young people are different. Their own evidence of attainment in the form of essays, drawings, accounts of sporting successes or the presentation of scientific problems is convincing but so far largely unavailable. From the point of view of educational benefit, however, the more that can be done to interest young people in their own educational progress and in their own life chances while they are still at school, the better. Both students and teachers are trained in cynicism when they have to submit to a system which records only success in examinations but omits all reference to other aspects of human consequence.

When school students know some years before reaching school leaving age that the school statement to be given them at sixteen-plus will be based in part on their own evidence of study, attainment, interests and purposes, their motivation may well be harnessed to school endeavour. When school-teachers come to appreciate the value of co-operation with students in trying to meet what they see as their educational needs, they will help to monitor the individual's progress in positive terms. All this is clear to schools aready working on these lines.[28] What they lack is recognition through accreditation of records based on professional judgement. Only when local, regional and national arrangements can be made for accreditation of school statements will the recording of non-examinable characteristics and achievements be seriously undertaken in all schools.

The proposal is that schools build up a summary statement based on each student's progress through the two-year programme to which he or she was committed, taking into account both the evidence built up by the student, the records accumulated by the staff, the results of any graded tests or other competitions and the results of any public examinations. Draft statements will be scrutinized by members of an accrediting board which has access to the statements of intent to which each student gave his or her commitment.

This visiting accrediting board would not be the same as the validating board. Accredititation is an independent and distinct process and would be in the hands of a group of persons including, for instance, experienced teachers, university academics, members of the advisory service, examiners with the experience of Mode 3, personnel officers and research staff from the Manpower Services Commission. The recognition given by such a board to the statements produced in any school would be given national currency by a national accrediting body operating through a regional organization.

Each accrediting board would visit several schools, and each regional office would administer the work of a number of accrediting boards, sorting out disputes and judging standards. The national body would be comparable to the Council for National Academic Awards, but would be concerned with secondary school outcomes and the product of compulsory education.

The steps needed to establish the suggested framework begin in the school. A head and staff would agree to wanting to make a change in their reporting of the outcomes of education for their sixteen-year-olds in such a way as to lead to an improvement in the motivation of students of every kind. The head would then outline the proposal to his governing body and ask for a validating board to be set up. On the recommendation of a governing body, the local education authority would be likely to co-operate in establishing a suitable group. The good offices of local education authorities would also help in the setting up of a local accreditation board and in establishing its contacts with a national centre. At least during the experimental period, if not longer, the Royal Society of Arts itself would be prepared to act as the national accrediting body, ready to establish the arrangements locally, regionally and nationally.[29]

Developments along these lines will enhance the responsibility of school students and their parents; develop the professional competence and judgement of teachers; improve the proper accountability of schools and enable the education service to make a greater contribution to the capabilities of young people and improve their outlook at the point of transfer to the post-compulsory stage.

### References

1   MORTIMORE, J. and P. (1983). *Helpful Servants or Dominating Master: a critique of the secondary school examination system.* London: Inner London Education Authority.

PEARCE, J. (1972). *School Examinations.* London: Collier-Macmillan.

ADAMS, E. (1982). 'The 16 plus Examination System: England's Extravagant Anachronism'. In: *New Horizons in Education,* No.67. University of Sydney.

2 BELOE REPORT (1960) GREAT BRITAIN. DEPARTMENT OF EDUCATION AND SCIENCE. *Secondary School Examinations other than GCE.* London: HMSO.

3 Centre for the Study of Curriculum in Secondary Schools, Goodricke College, Heslington, University of York.

4 COVENTRY EDUCATION COMMITTEE (1983). *Comprehensive Education for Life.*

5 GREAT BRITAIN. MANPOWER SERVICES COMMISSION (1979). *Making Experience Work: principles and guidelines for providing work experience.*

6 GREAT BRITAIN. DEPARTMENT OF EDUCATION AND SCIENCE. FURTHER EDUCATION UNIT (1979). *A Basis for Choice: report of a study group of post-16 pre-employment courses.* London: FEU.

7 GREAT BRITAIN. MANPOWER SERVICES COMMISSION (1981). *A New Training Initiative, an agenda for action.* London: MSC.

8 *New Training Initiative Programme* (1981). White Paper. London: HMSO.

9 MSC and FEU (1982). *NTI Joint Statement.*

10 MRS/SSRC UNIT, UNIVERSITY OF SHEFFIELD (1981). *Young People Starting Work:* a report to the Training Services Division of the MSC and to the education authorities of Coventry, Leeds and Liverpool.

11 HAYES, C. *et al.* (1982). *Foundation Training Issues,* IMS Report 39. Institute of Manpower Studies, University of Sussex.

12 ADAMS, E. (1983). 'And Never the Twain Shall Meet', *Higher Education Review.* Croydon: Tyrrell Burgess Associates.

13 WARING, M. (1979). *Social Pressures and Curriculum Innovation: a study of the Nuffield Foundation Science Teaching Project.* London: Methuen.

14 Technical and Vocational Education Initiative (TVEI) for 14–18 year-olds in 14 pilot schools, 1983.

15 *Education 2000* (1983). Cambridge: Cambridge University Press.

16 GREAT BRITAIN. DEPARTMENT OF EDUCATION AND SCIENCE (1983). *The Work of HM Inspectorate in England and Wales: a Policy Statement by the Secretary of State for Education and Science and the Secretary of State for Wales.* London: HMSO.

17 BURGESS, T. AND ADAMS, E. (1980). *Outcomes of Education.* Basingstoke: Macmillan Education.

18 ADAMS, E., ROBBINS, and STEPHENS, (1981). *Validity and Validation in Higher Education.* Research report, North East London Polytechnic.

19   RAVEN, J. (1977). *Education, Values and Society. The Objectives of Education and the Nature and Development of Competence.* London: H K Lewis.
20   ADAMS, E. and BURGESS, T. (1981). *Statements at Sixteen: an Example.* Working Papers on Institutions No. 29. North East London Polytechnic.
21   DAVID, K. (1983). *Personal and Social Education in Secondary Schools.* London: Schools Council.
      GREAT BRITAIN. DEPARTMENT OF EDUCATION AND SCIENCE (1983) *Records of Achievements at 16:* Some examples of current practice, based on the visits of HMI to ten secondary schools in 1981 and 1983.
22   NATIONAL UNION OF TEACHERS (1983). *Pupil Profiles: a discussion document.* London: NUT.
23   BLACK, H. and BROADFOOT, P. (1982). *Keeping Track of Teaching: assessment in the modern classroom.* London: Routledge & Kegan Paul.
      SCOTTISH COUNCIL FOR RESEARCH IN EDUCATION (1977). *Pupils in Profile: making the most of teachers' knowledge of pupils.* Edinburgh: SCRE.
24   GOACHER, B. (1983). *Researching Achievement at 16 plus.* Harlow: Longmans for the Schools Council.
25   CITY AND GUILDS OF LONDON INSTITUTE. GREAT BRITAIN. MANPOWER SERVICES COMMISSION (1983). *An Evaluation of a Basic Abilities Profiling System across a range of Education and Training Provisions,* Interim Report. Sheffield: Manpower Services Commission.
26   CGL (1983). *A Survey of Vocational Gatekeepers' Opinions about Profile Reports,* Profiling Project 3. London: Manpower Services Commission.
27   NUTTAL, D. (1979). 'The Myth of Comparability,' In: *Journal of the National Association of Inspectors and Advisors,* No. 11.
28   MOON, B. (Ed) (1983). *Comprehensive Schools: Challenge and Change.* Windsor: NFER-NELSON
29   ROGERS, R. (1983). 'Going for Independence.' In: *Arts Express,* demonstration copy.

# CHAPTER 8
# Fostering Competence

*John Raven*

Most parents, teachers, students and employers agree[1] that education should foster such qualities as initiative, confidence in dealing with others, ability to analyse social systems, responsibility and leadership. This view of education is supported by studies which show that competent behaviour in almost any job – whether as milkman, machine operative or managing director of a multi-national corporation – demands such qualities.[2] In general, however, schools and colleges fail to foster these qualities[3] mainly because what happens in school is not determined by parents, teachers, employers or even Secretaries of State: it is determined by what is assessed when young people leave school; that is, at the point of interface between the educational system and society.[4]

The prevailing system of terminal assessment ensures that the attention of teachers and students has to be concentrated on preparing for examinations in the subject matter of particular courses of study. There are no similar means of giving students credit for having developed any of the qualities or components of competence that they will need at work; no means, either, of giving teachers credit for having fostered any of these desirable capabilities among students. This lack of formal recognition of the components of competence results in teachers being somewhat vague about the nature of these qualities and about how to foster them. My purpose in this chapter is to discuss the nature of competence and the processes through which it can be developed. The best way to start is to take a particular example, such as 'initiative'. The first thing to be noted is that it does not make sense to describe as 'initiative' any behaviour which the individual concerned has to be told to display. The self-motivated quality of the characteristic is integral to its nature. If one is to foster this quality one therefore has to foster in students the tendency to trigger it off for themselves. Next it should be noted that if an individual is to take a successful initiative he has to devote a great deal of time and thought to the activity. He has to build up and bring to bear a unique set of specialist knowledge – which is most unlike the low-level, general, out-of-date knowledge communicated to most students in most courses. He has to take innovative action, monitor the effects of the action, learn from those effects more about the problem he is tackling and the effectiveness of the strategies he is using. He has to wake up at night in an effort to seize on the flickering glimmerings of understanding on the fringe of consciousness and bring them to the centre of attention so that they become fully conscious and usable. He has to anticipate obstacles in the future and invent ways of circumventing them. He has to get the help of other people. No-one is going to do any of these things unless he cares very strongly indeed about the goal in pursuit of which he is attempting to display initiative. The valued goal is of crucial importance.

Values and intentions are thus crucial to fostering and assessing competence. Indeed, in view of the central role which assessment plays in determining educational activities, it is important to emphasize that it does not make sense to attempt to assess abilities except in relation to valued goals. This applies to cognitive development as much as to any other form of development.[5] People cannot be expected to develop competencies unless they arc practising them in pursuit of a goal which they care very much about. Educational programmes designed to foster competence must be individualized in relation to particular students' values and goals.

We are now in a position to say a little more about why it is that goals of this sort are so frequently neglected by schools. Again, the problem is probably best illustrated by taking an example. In a school we visited recently,[6] the teacher had engaged her pupils in a programme of environmental studies. One pupil had become expert on the distribution of different species of butterfly in the locality, another on the history of a particular agricultural implement, a third on the social structure of the area: who knew whom, and what they talked about.

It is hard to give credit in traditional ways for such idiosyncratic knowledge because separate scales would be needed for each individual. Moreover, the first pupil had developed the skills of the scientist – not a knowledge of science. The second had developed the self-motivated competencies and preoccupations required to be a historian, and the third had developed the competencies required to be a sociologist. Not only are traditional procedures unable to cope with the problem of idiosyncratic knowledge, they are even less able to credential the growth of the subtle skills, motivated habits, thoughtways and pre-occupations which go to make up the repertoire of the scientist, historian or sociologist.

Again, because the pupils had worked as a group, one pupil had become good at co-ordinating the activities of others, another at putting others at ease and smoothing over difficulties, another at presenting the results of other people's work to external visitors – a communicator rather than a scientist. These competencies are idiosyncratic and defy conventional measurement.

Not only was it impossible to testify to the development of these idiosyncratic pools of knowledge and areas of competence in such a way as to demonstrate to parents and directors of education that it was all worthwhile, it was also impossible for the teacher to plan individualized programmes of growth which ran from one year or one project to the next and which built on the particular areas of knowledge and competence which each pupil had developed. This means that new, individualized, competency-oriented assessment procedures are needed to enable teachers to implement and justify such activities and to credential pupils' growth in such a way that the pupils can claim credit for having developed competence when they come to compete for a job.

Two recent projects[7] have enabled us to advance greatly our understanding of the processes to be used to foster the components of competence. These build heavily on the composite accounts of such educational processes as project work and discussion lessons built up in previous work.[8]

Again, it may help to take an example. In order to achieve the broader goals of which we have spoken another teacher organized her entire programme of work around project-based, enquiry-oriented, activities, based in out-of-school visits. This not only made it possible for her to integrate traditional school subjects, it also permitted her to discover each of her pupils' distinctive interests and patterns of competence. These interests could lie either in the types of behaviour which made them enthusiastic (including, for example, such things as finding better ways of doing things, better ways of thinking about things, or getting a group of people to work together) or they could lie in particular content (such as Celtic civilization, the aerodynamics of aeroplanes or the distribution of particular species of tree). Not only was the teacher then able to promote the growth of many components of competence in relation to those interests, she was able to tap different interests and motivations on the part of different pupils to fuel enthusiasm for development activity in her classroom. In this way she created an overall climate of enthusiasm and dedication which infected other pupils. She was also able to tap multiple motivations to fuel the activities of any one pupil. Thus, a pupil might embark on a task for one reason, but be carried forward to complete it for another reason – because he was able, for example, to work with other children whose company he enjoyed. In this way, she was able to tap a wide variety of potential motivations, which are generally neglected in schools, both within and between pupils.

The teacher's own behaviour was itself a striking source of stimulation and growth for the pupils. She shared her thoughts and feelings with her pupils. She shared her planning and anticipations, her concern with excellence, innovation and efficiency, her disdain for petty regulations, her anticipation of obstacles and her search for ways round them, her concern with aesthetics, her feeling of being in control of her destiny. She demonstrated how to capitalize upon whatever resources were available – indeed to tailor her purposes to those resources instead of, as was characteristic of many other teachers, complaining about the lack of resources to do what they wanted to do. In these ways she communicated her values to her pupils and portrayed effective, competent, behaviour in such a way that they could emulate, not only the explicit behaviour, but the entire pattern of thinking and feeling which lay behind it. By eschewing the role of expert and provider of wisdom – by regularly trying to do things which she did not know how to do and tackling questions which she did not know how to answer – she showed her pupils how to be learners and how to innovate. By accepting pupils' suggestions she showed them that authorities and leaders are not best regarded as sources of information and organization, but as people who, at best, help other people to articulate and share what they know, acknowledge what others have contributed, and lead others to feel capable of achieving, and motivated to achieve, their own goals.

In a similar way her pupils learned a great deal from, and came to rely more extensively on, their fellow-pupils. They developed a partnership in learning. Aided by a vocabulary supplied by their teacher, they became able to think about, and value, the contributions of others who had not 'done as they were told'. The teacher herself would enlist the help of her pupils in trying to find ways of tapping the energies of other – perhaps in some ways disruptive – pupils. In this way, she both made explicit the fact that not everyone contributes in the same manner to a group process, and also the thought processes which contribute to effective leadership and management. By involving her pupils in this process she helped them to develop leadership and managerial skills.

There can be no doubt that through these processes the pupils learned to value beauty and efficiency. They learned to value other people who had different values, pre-occupations and abilities. They learned to value research, and to link research with improvement in the quality of everyday life. They learned to treat bureaucratic rules as guidelines rather than as requirements. They learned to exercise discretion, to lead, to investigate, to build up their own picture of the world from scraps of information. They learned how to work out implications of that picture for their own behaviour and how to take the initiative required to act on such personal understanding. They learned how to ask questions rather than only how to answer them, and they came to think that it was appropriate for people like themselves to ask questions instead of answer them. They learned to discuss, to speak effectively, to learn from others, and to communicate to others through artistic and graphic material, by allusion and presentation, and by gestures. They learned that they themselves were competent to learn on their own, that they were competent to invent, to have opinions, and to contribute ideas. They became less likely than other pupils to develop feelings of 'trained incapacity' – feelings of inability to do anything until one had mastered a vast array of material. They learned that they could become experts in any area they chose relatively easily. Learning itself was de-mystified.

In classroom activities based on the pupils' out-of-school studies, this teacher encouraged her pupils to set historical material in its social and economic context. Although she might have done more to lead her pupils to develop the habit of studying the workings of social, political and economic systems, she did encourage them to find out about the way of life of peoples who lived at previous times and, in so doing, encouraged them to focus on certain features of social and economic systems. The pupils read, and were read to, about the pre-occupations, perceptions, and thought-ways of people of past ages, and heard about the social consequences of those values, pre-occupations and thoughtways: they practised thinking in these ways themselves; and they made up stories in which they tried to get into the skins of people from a bygone age. They undoubtedly learned a great deal about social and economic processes: 'The Druids changed sides and became priests in the Roman Temples.' (Nevertheless, what they learned might benefit from more systematic consideration.) The pupils practised building up a picture of society and its structure from scraps of information, and were thereby discouraged from believing that one's first task is to get an authoritative version of events.

While the above example is taken from primary school work, Winter and McClelland, in an outstanding study of Ivy League and other colleges in the United States, have shown that the same processes operate there. The course content is not important. Neither is residential experience. What is important is participating in challenging activities which demand high levels of initiative, self confidence, leadership and specialist knowledge. Few universities both provide opportunities for, and attach great importance to, such activities.

We can now abstract from this discussion the features of developmental environments which can be used to develop competence. They include:

An opportunity to practise the components of competence in relation to a goal which one cares very strongly about.

A warm, honest, responsive, supportive climate which encourages experiment and innovation, which seeks out and recognizes that which is worthwhile in what one has done, and which does not focus on rule-following conformity in relation to pedants' rules, or penalize mistakes and omissions.

A climate which permits and encourages value-clarification and the resolution of value conflicts.

A climate which encourages one to reflect on the value of the goals one is pursuing and allows one to reject and neglect the trivial and the pointless.

A climate which sets and expects high standards, enthusiasm and making the most of oneself, and which is prepared to recognise as valuable and outstanding a wide range of different types of contribution.

Opportunities to observe the normally private, patterns of thinking and feeling which characterize competent behaviour in others. This is best done in relation to others whose values one shares. (This points toward de-registration in teaching and the development of case history material to portray the thinking, feeling, and behavioural components of effective behaviour in relation to a wide range of different values.)

Creation of opportunities to practise the components of competence in relation to a wide range of valued goals so that one can perfect one's habits and strategies, and try the valued behaviours for 'fit' without the consequences being too serious. (This points to the need to create educational games and simulation exercises.) It is particularly important to enable students to experience the patterns of satisfaction and frustration which are associated with the pursuit of different value-laden ends.

Support by adults who see themselves as 'facilitators of growth', rather than as teachers. That is, support by adults who respect individual students' values and talents and define their jobs as being to surface and recognize the value of such diverse values and talents rather than as being to convey standard, prescribed, information to large groups of students.

It is possible for effective developmental environments to vary in their degree of structure from being relatively unstructured (such as inquiry-oriented, project-based, 'methods' of education) to highly structured programmes designed to promote value clarification and the development of particular motivational dispositions.[9]

The promotion of competence also has wider social implications. In the course of our work we discovered that incompetent behaviour frequently resulted from disfunctional beliefs about the way organizations, the economic system and the political system did, and should, work, and one's own role in them. Thus, people most often did not communicate, not because they were inarticulate, but because they, their colleagues, and their managers thought that it was inappropriate for anyone in their position to have, let alone articulate, any opinions. They did not try to influence what happened in their society, not because they would have been incapable of doing so, but because they thought it was wrong for someone in their position to try to do so. They did not try to influence the wider social system which primarily determined their effectiveness at work because they thought that it was not part of their job to do so. They did not try to initiate the activities which needed to be undertaken to improve the quality of their lives because they believed that 'there was no money available to do so.'

The rôle which perceptions and understandings of a large number of concepts which deal with politics, social relationships, and institutional arrangements play in controlling the release of competent behaviour has only gradually emerged in our research. A few examples of the relevant concepts are the following:

*politics* ('a dirty, underhand business in which no self-respecting citizen would engage'); *participation* ('sitting on committees'); *democracy* ('the right of the majority to take decisions which will be binding on all' rather than 'the art of finding ways of enabling different sub-groups in the population to pursue their own values'); *equality* ('the same thing for everyone' rather than 'equal access to differentiated treatment'); *accountability* (only upward); *and wealth* ('something which one must have before one can do anything' rather than 'a product of organised activity').[10]

The development and release of competent behaviour is, therefore, not only dependent on fostering value-laden competencies in relation to personal interests and intentions, but also dependent on communicating to students new understandings of concepts such as these. One way in which this can be done is to encourage them to undertake organizational – and community – self-surveys which lead them to examine the probable consequences of shared perceptions, expectations and beliefs. (A set of questionnaires (*The Edinburgh Questionnaires*) is available in published form for use with adults in such studies.)

We are now in a position to summarize what we have learned

about the nature of competence. The main components of competence include:

*Self-motivated, value-laden, qualities or competencies.* These include characteristics like initiative, leadership, and the spontaneous tendency to observe the way our organizations and society work and think out the implications for one's own behaviour. All of these qualities are heavily dependent on idiosyncratic, specialist, knowledge – not out-of-date, non-specialist, general knowledge of which courses and educational programmes tend primarily to consist.

*Perceptions and expectations relating to the way society works, and one's own role in that structure.* Under this heading we may include such things as peoples' self images, the way they think their organizations work and their own role and that of others in those organizations, their understanding of organizational social climates which make for innovation, responsibility, and development rather than stagnation, and their perceptions of the reference points which it is appropriate to adopt in their quest for the understandings they need to guide their behaviour.

*Peoples' understandings of what is meant by a number of terms which describe relationships within organizations:* terms like leadership, decision-taking, democracy, equality, responsibility, accountability and delegation.

A fair amount is now known about the nature of competence and how to foster the development of its components. Apart from the political problem of legitimizing the pursuit of variety, and dealing with value-laden education and political issues, the problems now are:

1  that what happens in schools is primarily determined by what is assessed at the point of interface between schools and society; and,

2  that, if competence-based education programmes are to be implemented effectively, teachers need tools which will enable them to assess pupils' values and interests and to implement competence-based educational programmes in relation to those interests and values.

The theoretical and practical bases on which it would be possible to build assessment devices both to give students credit for the competencies they have developed and to administer individualised, competency-oriented programmes of growth are now available.[11]

However, there are two important conclusions to which attention must be drawn here. The first is that, in the light of what we have seen, it is obvious that these qualities cannot be meaningfully assessed except in relation to pupils' values and intentions. Put the other way round, the assessment of values, motives and intentions must play a dominant role in assessment. Second, it does not make sense to attempt to assess these qualities in 'educational' environments in which pupils have had no opportunity to develop them. Thus, if the urgently needed new forms of assessment are to be developed, it is essential that they be developed through theoretically-based action-research programmes which are concerned both with curriculum development and assessment. In the past, those responsible for curriculum development and examinations have recoiled from forging this line.[12]

**References**

1   JOHNSTON, L.D. and BACHMAN, J.G. (1976), 'Educational Institutions'. *In* ADAMS, J.F., *Understanding Adolescence,* IIIrd edition. Boston: Allyn & Bacon, p.290–315.
   MACBEATH, J., MEARNS, D., THOMSON, B. and HOW, S. (1981). *Social Education: The Scottish Approach.* Jordanhill College of Education, Glasgow.
   RAVEN, J. (1977). *Education, Values and Society: The Objectives of Education and the Nature and Development of Competence.* London: H K Lewis; New York: The Psychological Corporation.
2   KLEMP, G.O., MUNGER, M.T. and SPENCER, L.M. (1977). *An Analysis of Leadership and Management Competencies of Commissioned and Non-Commissioned Naval Officers in the Pacific and Atlantic Fleets.* Boston: McBer.
   RAVEN, J. (1977). op cit.
   RAVEN, J. (1984). *Competence in Modern Society,* London: H K Lewis.
   FLANAGAN, J.C. (1983). 'The Contribution of Educational Institutions to the Quality of Life of Americans', *International Review of Applied Psychology,* 32, p.275–88.
   SPENCER, L.M. (1983). *Soft Skill Competencies.* Edinburgh: The Scottish Council for Research in Education.
   WINTER, D.G., MCCLELLAND, D.C. and STEWART, A.J. (1981). *A New Case for the Liberal Arts.* California: Jossey-Bass.

3  BACHMAN, J.G., O'MALLEY, P.M. and JOHNSTON, L.D. (1979). *Adolescence to Adulthood: Change and Stability in the Lives of Young Men.* Institute of Social Research, Ann Arbor.
   FLANAGAN, J.C. (Ed) (1978). *Perspectives on Improving Education.* New York: Praeger Publishers.
   GOW, L. and MCPHERSON, A. (Eds) (1980). *Tell Them From Me: Scottish School Leavers write about School and Life Afterwards.* Aberdeen University Press.
   GRAY, J., MCPHERSON, A. and RAFFE, D. (1983). *Reconstructions of Secondary Education: Theory and Practice Since the War.* London: Routledge & Kegan Paul.
   HMI (Scotland) (1980). *Learning and Teaching in Primary 4 and Primary 7.* Edinburgh: HMSO.
   MACBEATH *et al., op cit.*
   RAVEN, J. (1977), *op cit.*
   RAVEN, J., JOHNSTONE J. and VARLEY, T. (1985). *Opening the Primary Classroom.* Edinburgh: The Scottish Council for Research in Education.
4  RAVEN, J. (1977), *op cit.*
   BROADFOOT, P. (1979). *Assessment, Schools and Society.* London: Methuen.
5  FLANAGAN, J.C. (1978), *op cit.*
   RAVEN, J. (1980). *Parents, Teachers and Children.* Edinburgh: The Scottish Council for Research in Education.
6  RAVEN, JOHNSTONE and VARLEY (1985), *op cit.*
7  RAVEN (1980), *op cit.*, RAVEN (1985) *op cit.*
8  RAVEN (1977), *op cit.*
9  RAVEN (1977), *op cit.*
10 RAVEN, J., WHELAN, C.T., PFRETZSCHNER, P.A. and BOROCK, D.M. (1976), *Political Culture in Ireland: The Views of Two Generations.* Dublin: The Institute of Public Administration.
   RAVEN, J. and LITTON, F. (1976), 'Irish Pupils' Civic Attitudes', *Oideas*, 16, p.16–30.
   RAVEN, J. (1980), 'Teetering on the Brink of a Totalitarian Society?', *New University Quarterly*, 34, p.370–82.
   RAVEN, J. (1983), 'Towards New Concepts and Institutions in Modern Society', *New Universities Quarterly*, 37, p.100–118.
   RAVEN (1984), *op cit.*
11 BURGESS, T. and ADAMS, E.A. (1980). *Outcomes of Education.* London: Macmillan Education.
   RAVEN (1984), *op cit.*
   RAVEN, J. and VARLEY, T. (1984). 'Some Classrooms and their Effects', *Collected Original Resources in Education*, March 1984.
12 ADAMS, E.A. (1983), 'And Never the Twain Shall Meet: the Schools Council', *Higher Education Review*, Summer 1983, p.38–53.

# CHAPTER 9
# Engineering for Capability
*John Pratt*

The case for education for capability, as an education developing competence, co-operation and creativity, has often been taken to imply the encouragement of practical and vocational courses. In particular it is thought that courses in practical subjects, like engineering, would almost automatically qualify for 'recognition' under the Education for Capability scheme, since they could be said to be devoted to making and doing. There are three reasons why this view is mistaken. The first is that existing engineering education is as corrupted by the scholastic tradition as any other part of education. The second is that, like those with any other qualification, engineers need to be capable *persons*, not just capable professionals. The third is that there are characteristics of engineering as an activity that should form part of everyone's education for capability. Education for capability is as much of a challenge to engineering education as to any other.

The corruption of existing engineering education is a deep-rooted problem for it derives not just from educational practice – and theory – but also from commonly perceived views of the nature of society and the place of a practical culture within it. We could do worse than remind ourselves of what the Finniston Committee on the Engineering Profession had to say about the place of engineering in Britain and British culture.[1]

The Committee's report began with an energetic rebuff to those who argued that Britain was becoming a post-industrial society and therefore should concentrate on service industries rather than manufacturing. It showed that manufacturing occupies a key and irreplaceable place in the economy. At the time, it produced 30 per cent of the nation's wealth and employed 32 per cent of the working population, whilst probably half of those employed in non-manufacturing sectors depended for their jobs on links with manufacturing. Two thirds of goods and services exported were contributed by manufacturing industry, and to replace a one per cent fall in export earnings from manufacturing would require a 2.5 per cent increase in earnings from services.

Nor is the importance of engineering restricted to manufacturing industry, proportions of GNP or the balance of trade. It dominates our lives; we meet the results of the engineer's work everywhere every day. Engineering helps us to work and eat, it offers shelter, transport and recreation; it disposes of the waste we produce. It is almost impossible to understate the role of engineering in human development. Engineers have been called 'the makers of modern civilisation'[2] and the history of engineering regarded as 'coincidental with the history of civilisation.'[3]

Yet an opinion poll in 1978 showed that one fifth of respondents expressed complete ignorance of what engineers do and over two thirds perceived an engineer as someone doing 'manual work'. The status of engineering in the country is dismal. Finniston said:

'There have been neither the cultural nor the pecuniary rewards in this country to attract sufficient of the brightest national talents into engineering . . . Great prestige is attached to science, medicine and the creative arts . . . but there is no cultural equivalent in Britain, and hence no basis for according similar esteem, to the European concepts conveyed in German by 'technik' – the synthesis of knowledge from many disciplines to devise technical and economical solutions to practical problems.'

In Finniston's view, a large part of the blame for this lay in 'the national tendency to regard engineering as a subordinate branch of "science"', for which tendency the education system was much to blame.

The subordination of engineering to science – the view that it is an 'applied' science (whilst science itself is 'pure') – does not stand up in either theory or practice. If differs from science in purpose, output and process, though shares one fundamental component in logic. Science is concerned with creation of knowledge. As Sir Brian Flowers put it, [4] 'Its proper though restricted meaning is the growing body of coherent knowledge of the nature and behaviour of the physical universe, including man himself.' In terms more familiar to those concerned with Education for Capability, Flowers went on: 'It is a branch of knowledge structured to answering the question "Why?" ' By contrast, engineering is concerned with the question 'How?'

This means, as Michael Fores has argued,[5] that engineering is in some ways not only different from, but the opposite of science. As he puts it, the scientist aims to break up the environment he observes into component parts so as to understand it; the engineer puts together bits of the environment to produce an artifact which suits a particular purpose. Fores says: 'The engineer is obsessed with the artificial and making it; whereas the natural scientist is obsessed with the natural and unmaking it. The engineer takes a heap of rubble and makes it an object of value. The scientist finds an object and makes it into rubble to understand its properties. Each mode of work is quite legitimate and each is well worth pursuing . . .'

The differences in output or product of the two processes are, at one level, obvious. Typically the output of science is knowledge; engineers typically produce three dimensional useful artifacts – physical devices. But at a more subtle level there is another fundamental difference: the scientist aims for the truth (even if it is not attainable); for him there is a single right solution – however elusive. Sensible engineers do not believe in right, or even best solutions. They have to produce solutions within constraints of time and cost. They have to produce things that work at the right time at the right price: they do not in fact have even to understand why they work. Nor can there be a best solution when the problems the engineer tackles are, like all real world problems, underspecified and the products will as likely as not be abused as much as used (who does not employ a screwdriver for opening a paint can?).

Nor is engineering simply the application of science to practical problems. Indeed as Ove Arup once wrote of a young engineer:[6] 'He realized that he wouldn't solve the world's problems, no matter how much science he studied: and he saw engineering in terms of problems that could be solved . . .' Of course, the engineer may make some use of science and its laws, but as Arup went on:

'In this (engineering) is more closely related to art or craft; as in art its problems are underspecified; there are many solutions, good, bad and indifferent. The art is, by the synthesis of ends and means, to arrive at a good solution. This is a creative activity, involving imagination, intuition and deliberate choice, for the possible solutions often vary in ways which cannot be directly compared by quantitative methods.'

The method of the engineer is that of trial and error because of the nature of the problems he tackles, however much science is available. For this reason it is a false dichotomy to divide the world into two cultures, art and science, for engineering is based on a third, encapsulated in continental Europe and elsewhere by the notion of 'technik'.

Technik is described by Finniston as 'the synthesis of knowledge from many disciplines to devise technical and economic solutions to practical problems.' It is well understood in continental Europe, in Japan and, to a lesser extent, in the USA where the engineer has a standing in his own right since his work is recongized as having social responsibility and economic value. 'Technik places everything taught firmly in the context of economic purpose.' Engineering is concerned with markets as much as with science; it is concerned with the solution of real problems rather than manipulation of knowledge. Technik encourages the idea that you have to run in order to stay still, for engineering involves technical change continuously. Nor is engineering 'management'; it involves managing certainly, but managing operations with a highly technical component. The line manager in production has to be a fire-fighter as much as a planner. What links all these disparate requirements of the engineer is the Technik concept, and more particularly the key technical function of design.

If the key to engineering is problem solving, then the key to problem solving is design. There is a design component to every technical function in engineering (and I would argue to most tasks in life), whether product development, the management of production, maintenance or repair. The design process has been variously described (and not all authorities agree on its precise characteristics; some even disagree that it exists at all, or if it does that it can be prescribed). What is clear is that there is a basic logic which underpins any attempt to solve engineering problems; it may not always be consciously followed, though things might be better if it was. It is a logic which engineering shares with science – their one fundamental similarity. (In science, too, it is not always recognized.) As in science, the logic starts with a problem, to which a solution is proposed; in engineering the solution is a physical device, in science it is a hypothesis; the solution is tested for failure; if it passes the test it is used until a better solution is found; and it leaves new problems for further solution.

One of the best accounts of the design process is given by Krick[7] (note, of course, that the author is American not British). He says, 'a discussion of engineering is essentially a discussion of problems and problem solving.' For him, a problem 'arises from the desire to achieve a transformation from one state of affairs to another.' The problem may be to get from one side of a river to another, or from poverty to wealth, or from ignorance to knowledge. What characterizes all problems is this existence of two states of affairs, the initial circumstances and the desired. What characterizes the problems that engineers tackle is that they are problems of the physical world, and typically the solutions are physical devices, machines, structures, systems. The first crucial stage of the problem solving process is thus the specification of these two states of affairs, problem formulation. Problem formulation is often neglected, in engineering as in many other aspects of life. Good engineering practice and good engineering education place special emphasis on it. For as Krick says: 'Rarely is the true problem laid before the engineer . . . its nature is ordinarily obscured by much irrelevant information, by solutions currently in use, by misleading opinions, and by unprofitable customary ways of viewing the problem.' All too often the engineer is required to build a solution, or proposes a solution before being clear what it is supposed to solve. Thus, in one of Krick's examples, an engineer is commissioned to design a multi-storey car park to reduce a severe parking problem. His task in the city's view is to do this economically and effectively in terms of structure and function. A good engineer will, however, ask to what problem is the car park a solution. Whilst it may solve the difficulty of cars blocking the streets, the car park may not be a good solution to the problem of transporting large number of people from their homes to their workplaces: or a bypass may relieve the congestion from transit vehicles.

Getting clear what the problem is, in broad detail-free terms, is the first characteristic of good engineering. Next comes analysis of the problem in more detail and the consideration of alternative solutions, which involves the engineer in considering a number of new factors. The important point here is that there is no one solution to any problem, nor even a best solution; but there can be a preferred solution. The preference is largely determined by the constraints that are imposed on the solution. These stages of the process are thus paradoxical, generating as many alternatives as possible, and eliminating many by consideration of constraints. A constraint on a solution is a characteristic of that solution which is previously fixed. Constraints can be many and various: cost, time, size, input or output capacity may all be restricted. Sometimes, constraints are unnecessary or fictitious: it may be assumed that the feed to a machine has to be in bags, whereas it need not be and a cheaper device results. A good engineer identifies the solution variables – the ways in which a solution can differ – and maximizes the range and combination of these; only then does he eliminate those which are justifiably constrained. The job of finding solutions is a matter of generating alternatives. For, as Krick says: 'Almost invariably there are a number of ways of accomplishing the specified objective' and the job of the engineer is 'to maximise the number and variety of solutions from which (he) can sample.' This requires two skills, because there are two sorts of solution: those already known and those which have to be invented. System is necessary to ensure that all known solutions have been considered; inventiveness generates new solutions.

The choice between the alternative solutions is made on the basis of criteria. These commonly include cost, safety, reliability, ease of maintenance, etc., though the weightings attached to each may vary. Indeed different emphasis among criteria can lead to opposing solutions. Safety usually points to one kind of solution, cost (or, rather, economy) to the opposite. Good engineers have to reconcile conflicting criteria.

The choice is made usually after the use of three important features of engineering practice. The first of these is the idea of testing. The effect of altering each of the solution variables on the criteria is examined in turn; alternative solutions are examined. Often the process involves the second feature, which is modelling; a way of predicting solution performance without the necessity of physically creating the solution. Models are small scale physical representations of the solution, or complex mathematical simulations, but they all have in common a description of the nature of behaviour, to the extent needed (and only to that extent), of some real life counterpart. Models are extensively used in engineering, not only for predictive testing, but also as aids to invention, for communication of ideas and as a control in building the actual solution (as in a blueprint). In testing the behaviour of a proposed solution the third feature of engineering practice, the concept of optimization, is frequently employed.

For most problems there is an optimum value of some criterion for some value of a solution variable. The difficulty is usually that other criteria reach their optima at different values. Much of the time of the engineer may be spent in the process of achieving a satisfactory balance between conflicting criteria. Optimization is a complex process of compromise. Most decisions have to be taken as a trade off; do you produce a cheap car with high operating costs or an expensive one with low running costs? Optimization usually involves the use of a model and an iterative process of trial and error; seeking to ascertain not only the optimum value of any variable, but also the sensitivity of the variable to changes of a manipulated variable. Like most things in engineering, the optimum is rarely attained. In practice it is usually a matter of seeking progressively better solutions until it becomes more profitable to spend the effort elsewhere. Judgements about this shift of emphasis are also part of the engineer's job.

The qualities needed in the engineer to undertake the tasks arc thus, as well as specific skills and knowledge, general competencies of the kind identified by John Raven in his chapter in this book, though interestingly in his main work on these issues[8] he does not discuss their development in the context of technical school subjects. Good engineers need to be proficient at sorting out problems from solutions; to have inquiring minds, to think about improving things and to be inventive in proposing new solutions; willing to use new ideas to achieve goals, challenge conventional wisdom about existing solutions; they need judgement, ability to use information resources, and to reach intelligent conclusions.

Unfortunately, the educational system, which fails to develop these capacities in general in its pupils and students fails in ı particular to develop them in engineers. The Finniston Committee recorded that engineering education had been 'the subject of a good deal of critical comment in previous reports and in the evidence to us'. The scholastic culture was dominant, for Finniston went on: 'Complaints commonly voiced, especially by employers, are that the education of engineers is unduly scientific and technical; that newly graduated engineers lack awareness of "real life" constraints to text book solutions; that they are orientated too much towards research and development work and are not interested in working in production or marketing functions; and that they lack understanding of the factors in the commercial success of their employing organisation.' Even the Committee of the Engineering Professors Conference agreed that 'most current first degree courses are not generally well matched to the requirements of industry.' The reason for this is, according to Finniston and many of those who gave evidence to the Committee, that engineering education in Britain, unlike that in many other countries, developed within the universities rather than in specialist institutions. The universities were historically founded 'upon the twin cultures of the liberal arts and pure science, and (engineering) was aligned with science to gain academic acceptance.' Thus, engineering courses have taught first underlying scientific theory, then the potential applications of it, building into engineering the fatal dichotomy between theory and practice.

There are of course exceptions to this sorry picture even in Britain. At school level, the development of Craft Design and Technology courses (CDT) has begun to challenge the conventional wisdom that technical subjects are basically inferior options for the manually gifted (or academically dull). These take an explicitly problem solving or design-based approach, offering pupils the opportunity to devise their own solutions to design problems, using a variety of materials. HMI summarized the aims of this approach as 'The acquisition of skills and cognitive development that gives girls and boys ability and confidence in identifying, examining and finally solving problems with the use of materials and tools.'[9] The importance of the subject is 'the quality of the pupils' total experience in designing, planning and testing . . . rather than the ability they may acquire in a specific competency.'[10] Thus an APU report on Design and Technology in schools contains a detailed assessment document for pupils identifying a large number of these basic competencies and skills. Similarly, at higher education level, engineering courses are beginning to recognize the importance of relating educational practice to the real world of engineering practice, and the importance of problem formulation and solving in this practice, as awards for Education for Capability show.

But the case for these kinds of developments in education is not restricted just to those who seek to become engineers. The competencies and skills that engineers employ are qualities and abilities that all pupils should have on completing their education. The characteristics of engineering problems – the transformation from one state of affairs to another – are characteristics of all real world practical problems; and the need to formulate problems before rushing to solutions, to be clear where we are now and which direction we would like to go in, the importance of eliminating unnecessary constraints on solutions, the value of appreciating that solutions are inevitably restricted by some constraints, the benefit of considering the variety of alternative solutions before opting for one, the acknowledgement that there are no best solutions, that there is a constant need to review and reform, to test and retest; all those are valuable parts of any individual's education and abilities to face the rest of his life. An education in engineering and education in other subjects based on engineering principles should be offered to all pupils.

It is not difficult to do this. Raven has shown how conventional school subjects can be taught in a way that generates the competencies and qualities he is concerned with. Even mathematics, that most abstract of disciplines, is susceptible, with thought, to application in ways of describing the world, and in the development of logical thought. Most subjects can similarly be taught in a way that makes clear the value of the discipline to the solution of practical problems, which are after all the main kinds of problems that pupils face now and in their later lives. Of course it will involve changes in teaching methods. Instead of cramming Ohm's law into reluctant minds sat in even rows, the process may involve project work on a problem of how to design a device to measure electric current. But much progress would be made if education was seen as offering answers to 'how' questions rather than 'why'.

## References

1  FINNISTON REPORT. GREAT BRITAIN. PARLIAMENT. HOUSE OF COMMONS. (1980). *Engineering our Future. Report of the Committee of Inquiry into the Engineering Profession.* London: HMSO.
2  SMILES, S. (1874). *Lives of the Engineers.* London: Murray, p. xxiii.
3  FLEMING, A.P.M. and BROCKLEBANK, H.J. (1925). *A History of Engineering.* London: A and C Black, p.1.
4  FLOWERS, SIR B. (1972). *Technology and Man.* Liverpool University Press.
5  FORES, M. (undated) Technology: A Tale told by a Fool. Manuscript.
6  'The World of the Structural Engineer' (1969). *Structural Engineer*, 47, pp.3–12.
7  KRICK, E.V. (1969). *An Introduction to Engineering and Engineering Design.* Chichester: John Wiley.
8  RAVEN, J. (1977). *Education, Values and Society.* London: H.K. Lewis.
9  GREAT BRITAIN. HER MAJESTY'S INSPECTORATE. DEPARTMENT OF EDUCATION AND SCIENCE (1980). *Craft, Design and Technology in Schools.* London: HMSO.
10  GREAT BRITAIN. DEPARTMENT OF EDUCATION AND SCIENCE (1981). *The School Curriculum.* London: HMSO.

# PART THREE:
# Solutions in Practice

# CHAPTER 10
# Education for Capability

*Peter Gorb*

Five years ago ten people pushed aside the coffee cups after a dinner at the London Business School and drafted the Manifesto (see p. *ix*). The backgrounds of these people were varied. They included industrialists, educators, a military historian, a psychologist and a civil servant. It was not easy for so disparate a group to agree the text of a manifesto; but they all held and hold the passionate belief that there is something seriously wrong with the British educational system, and that those wrongs are at the heart of the current malaise in British society, its miserable economic performance and its lack of industrial leadership.

At this point, if you have not already done so, I would like you to read the text of the Manifesto, and the list of those who have put their names to it: you may be surprised, as were the ten initiators, by the extent and quality of the support. Indeed, it quickly became clear that a movement had been started which was beyond the capacity of ten private individuals to manage. It was thus important for the growing movement that the Royal Society of Arts, true to its own traditions, should have taken over its administration. One of the first means chosen to further its ends was a 'recognition scheme', described in the next chapter by Timothy Cantell. The scheme attracted immediate interest – well over 600 inquiries in the first year alone, from industry, education, voluntary associations, government bodies and many others.

Since then the scheme has continued to arouse interest at all levels of education, from primary to post-graduate, from people involved in youth opportunity schemes to industrial training programmes.

There has also been a growing interest in Education for

Capability among those who make or influence educational policy, or who are concerned to do so. The Education for Capability committee has been asked (either collectively or individually) to address conferences, visit educational programmes, meet with local education authorities and respond to interest in the newspapers, journals and on radio and television. The continuing weight and quality of this response to what are, after all, not new educational ideas has, we think, two main causes.

The first is the timeliness of the message. When our informal group sat down to write the Education for Capability manifesto, they were aware that they were focusing a set of dissatisfactions that were common to many educators, industrialists and parents. The RSA provided a platform for three lectures by Correlli Barnett, Charles Handy and Tyrrell Burgess, which provided a background to the manifesto.

Economic decline, growing unemployment, the social alienation of young people, the cutbacks in education and the problems of its organization and control – all these issues served to reinforce the timeliness of the Education for Capability movement. In those early days, we were being carried forward on a tide of uneasiness about education and its place in society.

Another reason for the growing interest has been the home of the movement at the RSA. In introducing a symposium on the recognition scheme, Ian Hunter, the Chairman of the Council of the Society, touched on the eclectic nature of the Society's work, reflected in the audience, which included polytechnic directors and primary school children, managing directors and members of both Houses of Parliament. The RSA, as a wholly independent body, is a natural home for a movement which is trying to focus an educational debate spanning at least three departments of government and organizations from well outside the formal system of education. There are many worthwhile educational and related reform groups who wish to make connections with us, or to squeeze us into their mould. We therefore welcome every opportunity to restate our main concern, which is to correct a serious lack of balance in our education system. We wish to change the emphasis from a concentration on equipping young people for an 'academic life' to one which equips them for an 'active life'.

We have been accused of disparaging the 'academic', the pursuit of knowledge for its own sake, and the development of the cultivated individual, able to appreciate and evaluate and judge. It is not the case that we wish to abandon what Toby Weaver has encapsulated under the headings of Comprehension and Cultivation. But, as he said in introducing the discussion at the RSA symposium 'By themselves these two are not enough, except for scholars, critics and contemplatives.'

He went on to emphasize that a 'capably' educated person must learn how to exercise creative skills, to develop one or a number of special competencies, the 'know-how' on which modern society depends; and above all learn how to cope with the problems of life and work. Finally, all these things need to be done, not individually and competitively (as our examination systems demand), but by co-operative effort and joint action. We want young people to be prepared for a life of responsible action in a world where employers are concerned with what young people can do as well as what they know.

We take no sides in the debate about the pecking order of subjects. We believe all subjects should be taught with strong emphasis on their relevance to the lives of young people. We believe that young people need to learn how to identify and solve problems, and how to undertake and complete tasks using appropriate knowledge and skills. We believe they can learn to do this in nearly every subject area. It is, for example, sad to observe the extent to which technological subjects have all too often become fixed in an academic mould which, for example, treats engineering as an applied science.

Education for Capability should not be classified amongst the various 'understanding industry' schemes. We recognize the importance of these schemes in reinforcing the importance of wealth creation to new generations of school children. We also admire the attempt to place the relevance of work at the heart of the educational process.

But understanding by itself is not enough, even if it succeeds in creating among the young an admiration for the world of industry and commerce, and a desire to work within it. Effective performance in industry (or indeed in any job) requires action as well as appreciation, and 'know-how' even more than knowledge.

Again, in the field of work and employment, Education for Capability has occasionally, and wrongly, been identified with schemes which attempt to prepare school leavers, and particularly unemployed school leavers, for jobs. It is, of course, sensitive to the social and economic problems which motivate these schemes, and it has recognized a number of effective and heartwarming programmes associated with them. Education for Capability is concerned with the employed as well as the unemployed. It is the capability of the employed which will determine whether or not our immediate economic ills can be cured.

This view about school leavers has led to further confusion, which would confine Education for Capability to those who are unable or unwilling to tackle the examination hurdles towards higher education. But it is often those who are best at passing examinations who are most in need of the kind of education we are advocating. It is they who will ultimately manage or influence our society. We are hardly likely to do well as a nation if our ablest members are not helped to become doers and makers, organizers and problem-solvers.

Furthermore, the present debate on employment has begun to recognize that employment as we understand it is not necessarily the only way to live a full life and make a contribution to the wealth of the community. Education for Capability may well be a prerequisite to making the kinds of economic, social and emotional adjustments to new and perhaps still unknown ways of living and working.

A criticism levelled at the group is that because we 'preach' rather than 'practise', we do not 'practise what we preach'. Certainly it is not the purpose or the place of the RSA to do more than encourage and motivate the activities of others. In the end it is the education system itself which must make the changes. But, by providing an independent focus and forum, the RSA hopes to be catalytic in helping this particular reform movement.

If schemes designed to enhance capability are to find a stronger place in our system, ways of assessing student performance and validating those assessments need not only be devised and implemented, but also given status and independence. An assessment of capability which complements and perhaps eventually takes precedence over traditional examinations needs to be sought by employers and those responsible for university admissions, as well as by teachers and parents and, of course, by the students themselves.

One of the most effective points at which to insert a lever for educational change is the admissions level to higher education. The shift from the academic to problem-based ways of learning needs to take place at the universities themselves, most of whose students will never become academics.

Education for Capability is becoming better known: the phrase has entered the language of educational discussion. Thanks partly to external funding its scope has greatly increased, particularly since the appointment of a fellow and a consultant. The rest of this part of the book offers the spur of example to the growing numbers of people for whom the message of the manifesto is urgent.

# CHAPTER 11
# The Scheme in Operation
*Timothy Cantell*

To seek to correct a seriously wrong emphasis in British education is to embark on an exercise which is unlikely to be brief or effortless. The Education for Capability Committee, which first met at the RSA in October 1979, was aware of the size of the task it had set itself. It could have approached the seriously wrong emphasis in a number of ways. It might have seen its task as simply one of preaching the message of capability and expecting to convert the unconverted by argument or fervour alone. It might have tried at once to press forward model courses, programmes or curricula which somehow educators would then have adopted forthwith.

The Committee, however, chose for its first major project the Education for Capability Recognition Scheme. Sensing perhaps that reform more often flows from example than missionary zeal, the Committee set out to identify and publicize programmes already in operation which were helping people to be capable. This pragmatic and empirical approach would give encouragement to those designing and running such programmes, and in turn encourage others to start programmes or to modify existing ones. The Recognition Scheme, the Committee hoped, would demonstrate that Education for Capability could be put into practice and would show what benefits could be expected when it was. Looking ahead, the Committee also entertained the hope that with a body of 'case law' it would in due course be able to speak more legitimately and cogently about the seriously wrong emphasis it had identified.

The Recognition Scheme was first run in 1980. To announce it, the Education for Capability manifesto (see page *ix*) and the list of signatories (see page 177) were published for the first time, appearing in *The Guardian* and *The Times* together with brief details of the Scheme. A fuller document, sent to those who inquired, explained that the objective was to encourage a wider understanding of the need for educational change by supporting existing schemes of work and publicizing them as widely as possible, and by acting as a clearing house for information about current activities.

Applications could be made by schools, colleges, youth organizations, industrial and commercial companies, the public services and any other bodies or organizations engaged in the education or training of people of any age. Applicants were asked for a statement of 2000 to 3000 words, prefaced by a summary, describing the programme, stating its purpose and reviewing its desired and actual outcomes. Sixty-nine submissions were made. From these, the Committee selected a shortlist to all of which a visit was made by members of the Committee. These visits, in which the whole Committee, working in pairs, was involved, gave the two members an opportunity to discuss the entry with the organizers and to see the programme in operation. Above all, the visits provided a chance for the Committee members to talk to the pupils, students or whoever had actually undertaken the programme to inquire about their view of the programme and to gain an impression of how far they were being helped to live and work more effectively.

The Education for Capability Committee then decided, in the light of the reports of the visits, to give recognition to fifteen projects. A Symposium was held at the Society's House at which Lord Caldecote, Chairman of Investors in Industry and a signatory of the manifesto, presented certificates to representatives (in most cases, educated as well as educators) of the recognized projects. Four of the fifteen gave a brief account of their programme (again with pupils and students to the fore) and a discussion of Education for Capability followed. The printed certificate stated simply that the Society, through the Education for Capability Recognition Scheme, recognized the particular programme, adding a citation. The moral value of recognition, it was hoped, was the stronger for being given by an institution of well-established independence with a record of over 200 years of, to quote its full title, 'the encouragement of Arts, Manufactures and Commerce.'

The Recognition Scheme was run similarly in 1981, 1982 and 1983; in the second, third and fourth years, seventy-six, sixty-six and forty-nine applications were made and eleven, seventeen and eleven projects respectively gained recognition. The Scheme had become well-established and respected and in 1984 the Committee made it clear that the Scheme would continue for a number of years. It had become the foundation stone of the developing Education for Capability campaign.

The 1984 Scheme, in fact, involved a development of the previous years in two respects: the criteria were stated more explicitly and the culminating event was broadened into a Recognition Day at which those gaining Recognition could display their work and converse with visitors and each other.

The criteria used in 1984 and repeated for the 1985 Recognition Scheme provide a concise guide to the educational change which the Committee wishes to bring about. The criteria spring from an amplification of the imbalance identified in the manifesto:

'It is the aim of Education for Capability to encourage and develop in people four capacities that are currently under-emphasized in our education system.'

The great majority of learners – whether pupils at school, students at universities, polytechnics or colleges, or adults still wanting to learn – are destined for a productive life of practical action. They are going to do things, design things, make things, organize things, for the most part in co-operation with other people. They need to improve their *Competence*, by the practice of skills and the use of knowledge; to *Cope* better with their own lives and the problems that confront them and society; to develop their *Creative* abilities; and, above all, to *Co-operate* with other people. It is these four capacities that we want to see encouraged and developed through Education for Capability.

The education system at present gives most of its emphasis to two other educational aims – the development of the abilities to acquire and record specialized knowledge and to appreciate the values inherent in our cultural heritage. We call their achievement *Comprehension* and *Cultivation*, respectively, which by themselves are not enough; even for those destined to pursue a life of scholarship or contemplation, they do not alone afford an adequate preparation for life in the outside world.

In evaluating programmes, the Committee will take account of the extent to which:
1 the demonstrated competence of the learners is increased, particularly through active methods of learning which develop the existing interests, skills and experience of the learners;
2 the capacity to cope is developed by encouraging learners to find solutions to problems which they have personally identified, in contexts relevant to their own lives;
3 the creative abilities of learners are drawn upon and expanded through doing, making and organising; and
4 learners are encouraged to get on with other people and to initiate and engage in co-operative activity.

In addition, the Committee will be concerned that programmes:
5 involve the learners, according to their maturity, in negotiating with their teachers what it is they need to learn;
6 are accessible to a wide range of learners;
7 include methods of assessing and giving recognition to successful performance which are appropriate to the nature of the activity undertaken; and
8 have been running long enough to demonstrate results.

The Committee will also look for:
9 the extent to which the aims and objectives of the programme are understood and accepted by learners and staff; and
10 a coherent programme design and evidence of effective execution.

With the completion of the 1984 round, the number of programmes and projects recognized rose to seventy-one.

Perhaps the most striking feature about the list of recognized projects is its variety. Of the seventy-one, twenty-seven are in schools (primary and secondary), twenty-five in further and higher education while the remaining nineteen cover voluntary organizations such as the YWCA and Community Service Volunteers and projects straddling conventional boundaries such as the integrated degree course instigated by GEC-Marconi Electronics. In terms of subject, the scope extends well beyond the allegedly practical fields (which some regard, wrongly, as the proper province of capability) to economic studies, mathematics and English while others have escaped from the traditional subject pattern altogether.

Again, some of the recognized schemes represent efforts to shift the emphasis within the mainstream of the educational system while others are outside it. Both are valuable but the relatively small number of courses recognized from the mainstream of secondary schools has been at once a disappointment and a measure of the task facing the Committee. The organizers of the courses or programmes within the system which gained recognition not infrequently have been educators finding themselves at odds with the conventional wisdom; recognition of their work has consequently been a counterweight to the pressure often felt from the heads of institutions, from the authorities and sometimes from parents to restore or redouble the pursuit of only academic goals.

Most of the projects awarded Recognition had received little publicity previously and the Recognition Scheme has helped to bring them to public attention. A brief statement about each project, prepared by its organizers, is given to the press when the results are announced and is available to the media, to educators or anyone interested thereafter. The body of examples of Education for Capability put into practice in a range of spheres and in different ways will increase in value as it builds up.

A complete list of the projects recognized through the RSA Education for Capability Recognition Scheme between 1980 and 1984 is given below. A number of the schemes recognized are described in the chapter which follows. Details of other recognized schemes and of the Recognition Scheme itself may be obtained from Education for Capability, The RSA, John Adam Street, Adelphi, London WC2N 6EZ.

In the early days of the Society of Arts (as it then was), in 1760, Doctor Johnson, an early member, said: 'The Public concurrence of the Society will give to a new Practice that Countenance which Novelty must always need.' Education for Capability may not be entirely novel but it does need a certain countenance. The public concurrence of the Recognition Scheme is intended to provide it.

**The Recognized Schemes**

The Integrated Humanities and Design Course at the Bosworth College, Leicester

The Five Day Programme at Brook School, Sheffield

The Burford Certificate Scheme at Burford School, Oxford

The Preparation for Life of ESN(M) Pupils at Coppenhall County High School, Crewe, Cheshire

The Knowsley Pre-Employment Project in the Knowsley Borough Education Department, Merseyside

The Primary Schools and Units 'Getting Results and Solving Problems' Programme in the Oldham Borough Education Department, Oldham, Lancashire

The Lifeskills Teaching Programme of the South Eastern Education and Library Board, Belfast

The Full-Time Transition to Work Course for Handicapped School Leavers in the Department of General Studies at Burton on Trent Technical College

A Course in the Techniques and Technology of the Hand Forming and Decoration of Glass at the Glass Centre, Dudley College of Technology, West Midlands

Sussex Certificate Social Service Course 'Working with Mentally Handicapped People in Different Settings' at the West Sussex Institute of Higher Education, Bognor Regis

The Thirty-Day Full-Time Course in Pre-Vocational Education for Qualified Teachers at Homerton College, Cambridge

The Design: Processes and Products Course, Faculty of Technology-Design Discipline at the Open University, Milton Keynes

The Graduate Enterprise Programme of the Scottish Enterprise Foundation at the University of Stirling

The BSc Course in Engineering Design and Appropriate Technology in the Department of Engineering at the University of Warwick

The Neighbourhood and Local Studies Programme at Newcastle Architecture Workshop Ltd, Newcastle upon Tyne

The Skinningrove Training Workshop Programme, Middlesborough, Cleveland

The Community and Voluntary Work Training Programme at Self Start, Swindon, Wiltshire

The Problem-Solving and Design Course at Airedale High School, Castleford, Yorkshire

The Design for Living Programme at Brentwood County High School, Brentwood, Essex

The Lower Sixth Form Programme at Cranford Community School, Hounslow, Middlesex

The Integrated Education Project in Rural Science at Dartmouth School, Dartmouth, Devon

The Foundation Course in Recreational and Creative Subjects at the Eden Valley School, Edenbridge, Kent

The General Studies Course at Long Road Sixth Form College, Cambridge

The Waldorf Preparation for Life Course at the Michael Hall Rudolf Steiner School, Forest Row, Sussex

The Solving Problems – Individual, Community and Environment – Course (Spice) at Walton High School, Walton-on-the-Hill, Staffordshire

The BEd Degree Course in Pre-Service Primary Teacher Education at Thames Polytechnic, Dartford, Kent

The Crosskeys Islwyn Challenge at Unit 7, Nine Mile Point, Cwmfelinfach, Gwent

The Social Skills Training Course for the Transition to Independent Accommodation of the Housing Support Team at the North Lambeth Day Centre, London

The Personal Achievement Course at the Arnewood School, New Milton, Hampshire

The Threshold Course at Longhill School, Rottingdean, Sussex

The Design/Technology Project at the Sidney Stringer School and Community College, Coventry; with the Work Preparation Programme at the Coventry Training Workshops (TOPSHOP)

The CSE Course in Community Studies at Westhill Academy, Skene, Aberdeenshire

The Career-Orientated Degree Programme at the College of Ripon & York St John, York

BA by Independent Study at the Crewe + Alsager College of Higher Education, Cheshire

The BECSEC Project (A Young Enterprise Scheme) at the West Bromwich College of Commerce and Technology, West Midlands

The Diploma of Higher Education Course at the School for Independent Study, North East London Polytechnic

First Year of the BSc Course in the Department of Chemical Engineering at Teesside Polytechnic

The HND Mathematical Modelling Unit in the Department of Mathematics and Statistics at Teesside Polytechnic

The Communication of Scientific Ideas Course in the Department of Humanities at the Imperial College of Science and Technology, London

The Development of University English Teaching (DUET) Project at the University of East Anglia

The Properties of Materials Course in the Department of Civil Engineering at Heriot-Watt University, Edinburgh

The Personal Development Programme for Production Managers in the Collaborative Studies Unit at the University of Salford

The Integrated Degree Course in Electrical/Electronic Engineering Instigated by GEC-Marconi Electronics, Chelmsford, Essex

Development Training at the Brathay Hall Trust, Cumbria

The New Work Ventures Course at Project Fullemploy, Clerkenwell, London

The 'Starting a New Business Programme' in the Enterprise Development Unit of URBED, London

The Work of Workshop 6 Limited, Sheffield

The Young Enterprise Scheme, Chatham

The Girls at Work Course organized by the YWCA in London

The Combined University/Practice Course in the Department of Architecture at Sheffield University

The Managerial Analysis Course in the Division of Economic Studies at Sheffield University

The Various Personal Record Schemes for Schoolchildren prepared by Mr Don Stansbury

The Tyne and Wear New Job Horizons Youth Programme, Wallsend

The Skills Programme of the De Lisle R.C. Comprehensive School, Loughborough

The Craft, Design and Technology Work of Helenswood School, Hastings

The Part-Time Postgraduate Course in Design and Manufacture at Heriot-Watt University, Edinburgh

The Schools Liaison Work of Metal Box Limited, Reading

The Work of the Open College, Belfast

Real Problem Solving in Mathematics Teaching at the Open University

The John Makepeace School for Craftsmen in Wood, Parnham, Dorset

Draft Guidelines for Building Education Projects Prepared by Sergei Kadleigh, Bristol

The Master of Science Degree Course in Environmental Resources at the University of Salford

The Educational Programme of Artlaw Services Ltd, London

The Postern Programme at Dartington Hall, Devon

The Service Away from Home Scheme Sponsored by Community Service Volunteers, London

Creative Problem-Solving in the Civil Engineering Degrees at Middlesex Polytechnic

The Portland Workshop Project at Portland Comprehensive School, Worksop, Nottinghamshire

Forest School Camps

Shire Training Workshops at Stroud, Gloucestershire

The Work of Lewknor Primary School, Oxfordshire

The Senior Work Project at Belstead Special School, Ipswich, Suffolk

# CHAPTER 12
# Capability in Practice:
# some examples

This chapter offers some examples of capability in practice. It consists of accounts of some of the programmes which have been recognized by the Royal Society of Arts under the recognition scheme described earlier. The accounts have been written by those responsible for the programmes and in some cases by the students who have participated in them. They have been chosen to give an impression of the scope and variety of recognized programmes. As the following accounts show, there is enough taking place in formal and informal education of all kinds and at all levels for us to be sure that the correction of the imbalance in British education is generally practicable.

**Contributions**

The various Personal Record schemes for schoolchildren prepared by Mr Don Stansbury, Springline Trust, Devon (1980)

The work of Lewknor Primary School, Oxfordshire (1981)

The Design/Technology project at the Sidney Stringer School and Community College, Coventry; with the Work Preparation Programme at the Coventry Training Workshops (TOPSHOP) (1982)

The CSE course in Community Studies at Westhill Academy, Skene, Aberdeenshire (1982)

The Diploma of Higher Education course at the School for Independent Study, North East London Polytechnic (1982)

The Properties of Materials course in the Department of Civil Engineering at Heriot-Watt University, Edinburgh (1982)

The Personal Development programme for Production Managers in the Collaborative Studies Unit at the University of Salford (1982)

The New Work Ventures course at Project Fullemploy, Clerkenwell, London (1982)

The Crosskeys Islwyn Challenge at Unit 7, Nine Mile Point, Cwmfelinfach, Gwent (1983)

# The Record of Personal Experience

*Don Stansbury, Hon. Sec., The Springline Educational Trust*

The Education for Capability movement presents an ideal. The Record of Personal Experience scheme attempts to give that ideal a form, a structure, a symbol, a process and product. It attempts to give a proper emphasis to the development of personal qualities. It invites young people to think about their strengths and their personal resources. It offers a system whereby they can develop those strengths by doing things for themselves in and out of school and it enables them to leave with a written record which is evidence both of what they have done and what they can do.

The Record of Personal Experience has considerably prospered since the RSA Award in 1981. Over sixty schools are now involved. The Springline Educational Trust has been established with premises in Totnes, Devon, to serve those schools and to carry forward this ideal.

During the fourth and fifth years of secondary education, pupils select the things they have done which they feel will show what they can do, and they record these items on high quality headed loose-leaf cards which then go into a prestigious gold-blocked four-post folder. They have a regular time each week to do this when they can also have the attention of an adult who has acquired the tutoring skills known to be essential for this activity.

The Record of Personal Experience is not a kind of profile. The difference is that a profile provides information on a set of predetermined items and it usually provides that information in a standardized form so that comparisons can be made. Given this purpose, profiling cannot be very different from any other system of examining or grading or reporting on pupils.

The Record of Personal Experience is different. The records do not have a predetermined shape but are as different as the people who compile them. The aim is to encourage young people to develop their strengths and that means accepting all the different capabilities and specialisms that young people can develop. For instance one of the boys who left school in 1983 left with a Record of Personal Experience that was solely concerned with his guinea pigs and his goats. During his recording time he thought about and wrote about his business of buying and selling, breeding and rearing, feeding and housing these animals. When he left school to work full time and self-employed on that business it was clear that preparation for that had to be a significant part of his education and recording made it so. Young people do need this time in school when they can sort out their strengths and decide what they can make out of their personal resources. Of course, particularly when they first start recording, many young people say they have no interests and never do anything of any significance. It often takes all the skill of an experienced tutor to persuade some young people that the ordinary things that anyone may do, like looking after children, being with people, making things, solving problems, creating wealth, having fun, can be full of significance. This may not be easy. One girl who said she had no interests and never did anything was living with her stepfather who never allowed her to be late back from school. He filled her evenings and weekends with housework and never allowed her to go out or to bring anyone home. Her tutor could not change that situation, but could help that girl to find something positive about herself and so help her to survive into a better situation.

Every record is different but any record will show the distinctive quality of recording. When pupils begin in the fourth year, the first thing they have to do is to tackle three cards. One girl chose as her task 'Helping my mum clean the house and do the shopping'. Her 'work' card was 'Looking after my mum and dad's friends' children', which was a regular evening baby-sitting commitment. Her interest card was 'Looking after my rabbits.' On her second stage she recorded a journey to South Africa, her membership of a table tennis club, cycling round the village, making a teddy bear, making a toy and more baby-sitting, housework and shopping. On the open stage she recorded doing her paper round, working in a hotel during the summer, helping her father to adjust the brakes on their car, going with her father to consider purchasing a second-hand caravan, cycling to work, learning to swim, and the visit of her Aunty Jean, Uncle John and Cousin Sue.

Some readers may want to dismiss all of this as quite unbearably trivial, but it is the ordinary fabric of a life and out of this a person is fashioning a rôle for herself, a sense of identity and a sense of worth. It is all a process of education. Ideas of what may or may not be trivial are very subjective and it could be argued that some of those activities, like looking after children or adjusting the brakes on a car may be less trivial than some of the tasks more solemnly undertaken in schools.

A boy who began recording in the autumn of 1981 took as his self-chosen task, turning hay for baling. He did it on his father's farm and he did it by driving a tractor for three days, eight hours a day. His interest was sport: rugby, soccer and cricket. His work was feeding 2600 month-old chicks and thirteen calves every day. He went on to record helping to lay $5000\text{ft}^2$ of concrete, helping to build a barn, learning to plough, digging out a swimming pool, moving earth, playing rugby for his school and cricket for his village, and going to the Young Farmers' Club. The children of farmers often receive a working education of this kind out of school. It is an important part of their education and the process of recording makes it a part of the whole, underlines its importance and recognizes that all these things are worth doing well.

When young people leave school they often face quite difficult problems. Teachers cannot remove those problems but they can help young people to come to terms with them. The process of recording enables young people to define and develop their strengths and to see what their real resources are. Recording can include the whole range of human capabilities and concerns. It suggests that the ordinary business of living can be full of significance and full of things that are worth doing well. It suggests that personal worth and status not only result from employment but come from being able and willing to do things and having a place in an adult world.

Teachers who have experience of this work believe that if every pupil in every secondary school had the opportunity of making a record of this kind before leaving school it would considerably improve the capacity of young people to make the best of themselves and their circumstances. It would also make education broader and more balanced and more concerned with the world outside school which is, after all, what school ought to be about.

# Lewknor Primary School

*Mervyn Benford, Head Teacher*

At Lewknor we have resolved that for the six years the children are with us they shall have as many opportunities to make real decisions about their daily lives as possible. There are, of course, organizational constraints, professional priorities and social demands. The children themselves are still immature. Our resolve is real, not lip-service.

First, we accord children a programme of work based on a time period, for most of them a week. The programme covers the basic skills subjects and is individually set and monitored by the teachers. There are built-in expectations and potential corrective sanctions if these are not met, but the responsibility is left with the children, who have to manage their work across several different forms (maths, language, handwriting for example), making decisions such as when to do what and for how long. They have to assess their work in relation to their targets (the quasi-management words reflect the skills of personal management we are training), choose where to sit, and with whom, and be sufficiently responsible to 'do enough' if not more.

Second, we devote a whole afternoon to work which the children have freely chosen to do. It can be of any character that we are prepared to recognize as useful education. They determine where, with whom, how long before a change, the extent of the work they intend to cover, the relationship between types of work. They must organize their materials, even bringing things from home if they need to. They have to establish systems of co-operation for sharing space such as kitchen, sandpit and computer for which there may be several bids. They have to consider contingencies such as rain.

Third, the teachers have introduced into their own project work with the children a similar philosophy of handing them as much of the decision-making and conduct of the work as possible. These groups are across the full four to eleven age range, and it is usual for sub-groups to be formed in which younger and older will be together, with the older having to serve as leaders and ensure that the younger are usefully employed. Of course we teachers have a close supervisory and supporting role but we consciously wish to develop in our children the skills of leadership and the essential tolerances and insights the good manager needs – often missing in British industrial practice. We take from our local study projects what the *children* may see. And we let them work out the ideas *they* have. It is in the doing that they learn. The end product will inevitably show their immaturity and inexperience, but they will have learned about something not on the timetable in most schools, and they will have learned more than may be apparent from the conventional school project.

We would say that we have been able to develop our approaches because we have surrendered something of our traditional selves as teachers. We have had to abandon specific notions of curriculum. We concentrate on what is worth learning and what *can* be learned, allowing for the curious and quite unique nature of young children, which requires strategies very much geared to individuals as well as to groups. We have had to abandon the notion of the teacher as the purveyor of learning, as even the agent of learning or the controller of the classroom. How else could we accept Sarah's statement that we shall draw maths from the churchyard by counting the (limitless) number of flints in the church building itself, when by our training and high qualification we should never have even thought of such an idea? Moreover, having set such a spirit afoot one soon discovers that one's professionalism is far from abandoned. One's knowledge and skills are still heavily tapped, but far more in tune with child reality and the real world. The over riding role as guide and support and counsellor and spur comes to the fore as the dictator and instructor recede.

Finally, one must acknowledge that underpinning the entire structure (for there is a very real and constantly evaluated structure to our operations) is a commitment to education as a social experience for a social outcome. Ours is very much the real family atmosphere, and a real community spirit. Sadly, the bulk of schooling is undertaken in places as far removed from those vital pillars of individual security (even more vital when one is young and very small) as administrative myopia and prejudice can make them. One goes away to school, as to hospital. They are often aimless and alien places, remote from the real world and from real life. Perhaps that is part of the reality of being a student. But need it be? Would we not fit better into society at the end of education if we had always been a part of it and been educated in an atmosphere that reflected home and community values? Ours is very much a community school. Thus there is much scope for minds to be busy even if schoolwork palls for a moment or two. That can happen at Lewknor and be valued.

# The Design/Technology Project at the Sidney Stringer School; and the Work Preparation Programme at TOPSHOP

The Department of Education and Science Green Paper (1977) and the Working Paper published by the Coventry LEA recognized the need to introduce a higher degree of work relatedness into Coventry's school curriculum. It was thought important that the core curriculum in schools should be designed to correspond more closely with the needs of industry. This conclusion was further reinforced in a major study undertaken jointly by the Manpower Services Commission and the Coventry LEA the following year. 'The Coventry Report', as it came to be known, investigated the future education and training requirements of the City's population. It established that the local economy was undergoing a transformation and that future employment prospects in the City, which only a decade earlier had been a major boom town, were in sharp decline.

The LEA, concerned by the projection of rising youth unemployment, embarked upon a radical programme of work-related curriculum development in a bid to reduce the barriers which would confront inexperienced and unqualified school leavers when attempting to enter the labour market.

As a result of the report the LEA developed a strategy which aimed to equip the City's youth to achieve a smoother transition from school to adult life and possible employment. It consisted of two elements which came to be known as the 16− School Based Work Preparation Programme and the 16+ Youth Programme for school leavers.

After a number of pilot initiatives the Coventry Training Workshops were established in 1979. TOPSHOP, as the project came to be known, operated on three sites and offered up to 1500 training places, of which more than 400 were allocated to the 14–16 Programme.

The main aims of the TOPSHOP 14–16 project were to:
enable the pupil to experience both the vocational and social requirements of the world of work;
reinforce the schools' personal development, careers and academic programmes by relating them directly to the work situation, thus increasing the pupils' motivation;
enable the pupil to sample a type of work;
increase the pupils' awareness of employers' requirements, which may include: reliability, punctuality, self-discipline, interest and willingness to work;
develop the pupils' understanding of the company structure, role of management, trade unions and relationships at work;
encourage the active participation of school staff in the development of the programme;
inform the pupil of further training and education which may help meet the challenge of industrial and commercial life;
motivate the pupil by demonstrating the importance of mathematical and communication skills and the need for appropriate academic qualifications for entry into certain areas of industry and commerce.

It was also intended that the project would relate directly to certain academic courses; examples included understanding industrial society, design and technology.

In order to ensure that the experience offered to students became an integral part of the school curriculum, a central co-ordinating team was established and based at TOPSHOP. It was headed by a team leader who was supported by three specially seconded teachers, each of whom took responsibility for a group of work areas as well as a number of schools. Each school designated a deputy head or senior teacher to liaise with the TOPSHOP Team.

The programme consisted of three related stages:

preparation at school which included identifying projects, defining learning objectives and briefing students;
a two-week TOPSHOP-based education experience
a student de-briefing on return to school.

The pre-skill training opportunities which were made available to students took the form of self-contained workshops which specialized in the following areas of activity: painting and decoration, brickwork, woodwork, office work, fabrication, tubular work, plastics work, retail, motor vehicle maintenance and servicing, mechanical engineering, motor cycle maintenance and servicing.

In addition, a small number of placements were also arranged in workshops more directly committed to the 16–19 Programme. These placements included: office work, graphics, catering, design, Radio TOPSHOP, canal boat construction and audio-visual.

In order to provide such a broad range of activity a qualified and experienced team with an empathy with young people were appointed as School-TOPSHOP 'craftspersons'. This team was responsible for supervising, instructing and assessing the performance of students whilst on placement and was encouraged to participate in on-going in-service training programmes.

During the early stages of the programme a standard 'package' was provided for all students to choose their own work area. As the project developed, however, specific programmes were arranged to meet the requirements of individual schools and a range of flexible packages was offered. Some examples of these were:

problem solving and diagnostic testing in the motor vehicle area;

pre-skill training in the mechanical engineering workshop;

team work in the planning, designing and construction of canoes for students;

practical programmes on the effect of high technology in the work area;

planning, designing and producing a personal alarm system for the use of old age pensioners in the community;

exploring company structures and communication in the work area;

investigating the role and contribution of trade unions in industrial organizations.

These programmes now form part of the broader educational approach for all fourteen to sixteen year olds, and the opportunity for students from special schools to work alongside their peers from the secondary sector in a 'controlled work area'.

It may be helpful for readers interested in the project to consider some of the following major thrusts crucial to its development:

> consultation with all parties before implementation (students, parents, teachers, industrialists and trades unionists);
> policy of involving *all* students across the academic ability range;
> appointment of senior staff dedicated to the programme and committed to achieving its objectives;
> flexible and adaptable programmes designed to meet the needs of all schools individually;
> on-going in-service programmes arranged for the shop-floor staff;
> active support from industry;
> senior teachers designated as liaison teachers to ensure that the programme became an integral part of the in-school curriculum.

During their two weeks' experience, students were given the opportunity of experiencing the factors involved in the transition from school life to adult life which might include the world of work. These factors included: regular attendance, good time-keeping, relationships at work with the craftspersons and with their peers, understanding the reason for discipline and self-control in the work area, communication skills at work, management structure and the organization and rôle of the trade unions, practical problem-solving in the work area, working with adults, team work, experience of one-off, batch and line production, incentives and pride in the job, attitudes and willingness to work, attitude to safety, and need for an adaptable and flexible work force and equal opportunities in the work place.

It is probably still too early to assess the impact which the TOPSHOP school-based programme has had on the school curriculum. Dr Ian Jamieson (who was invited by the LEA to evaluate the programme) said:

'School TOPSHOP in Coventry remains a bold and imaginative experiment of education in an industrial setting. It will never be "realistic" enough for some; it will remain too industrial and vocational for others; on its present scale it will seem too ambitious and expensive for many LEAs. Yet the keynote of TOPSHOP has been adaptability and flexibility and that is the most important message to learn from the experiment.'

From our own internal feedback the programme has had an impact on the thinking of many teachers, who have seen their students in a different environment where the emphasis has been on co-operation and group work. The recognition by lower attaining academic students that knowledge and learning need not necessarily be associated with or assessed by examination performance has resulted in a positive change in attitude and many have discovered new capabilities and gained fresh insights which they take with them when they return to school.

# Westhill Academy's Community and Social Education Course

*Peter R Gibson, Rector*

The opening of Westhill Academy as a new school (defined as a community school) in a new town gave us the rare opportunity to attempt to build into our curriculum and methodology from the start some of those themes and skills prized by a changing society but gaining no toe-hold in the established schools. 'I need every minute as it is,' was the established subject's cry. Our compulsory course in community and social education was one way we attempted to help better to prepare all of our pupils for living in their own and external society by providing them with opportunities to understand the full range of their own needs and of their responsibilities to others using, wherever possible, experience from outside the school, and a manner of teaching not usually available to academic learning.

The course is compulsory during the four compulsory years of secondary schooling. In the first and second of these years, it is pursued from 9.00 to 9.30 am daily in the care of the pupil's tutor. In the third and fourth years, the course is one of only three compulsions of the core curriculum, the other two being mathematics and English. The pupils have seven other subjects, freely chosen, and so this course occupies one tenth of their work and is funded accordingly. In these third and fourth years, the course finds its major focus because these are the years of transition to life and work (or unemployment) in society after the school leaving-age. Thereafter students volunteering to continue with schooling may study the City and Guilds course in community care or are encouraged to consider a half day per week of community-work experience.

The major features of the course are the use of places of community care of the young, the old, the handicapped, and places of work to provide our pupils with external experience; the use of speakers from a wide range of community agencies, whose contributions are recorded on audio or video tape or in print for recurring reference; and the use of teachers from all of the subject disciplines so that the course does not become equated with any single subject and over-specialization.

Above all, a fresh set of methods of teaching is encouraged. The teacher's major responsibility is so to arrange matters that the pupils have to think and act for themselves and in co-operative groups. Listening and talking skills are given prominence in paired work, group work, and in full class discussion. Relevant problem-solving exercises are sought for the pupils to develop independent, co-operative, and creative thought. Variety of experience within the classroom and without is planned: the half-day unit of teaching time in the third and fourth years facilitates this aim. The teacher has to be skilled in providing and managing differentiated reading and writing tasks so that in the third of the course devoted to these areas pupils may work to capacity at their own pace and level in mixed-ability groupings. The mixed-ability groupings are themselves a guarantee of the natural community of society which the course is designed to explore.

When the pupils are assessed, equal weight is given over the third and fourth years to each of project or writing assignments of the pupil's own choice, aural/oral skills, and co-operative skills (shown in practical placements and in the classroom). Fourth-year achievements are given more weighting than third. The assessment in both years is continuous rather than by a large-scale examination at the end of each year. Mode 3 certification from the North Regional Examinations Board, Newcastle, is provided. The development in Scotland for a 1983 commencement of a course in social and vocational skills examined by the Scottish Examination Board has not impressed us to change boards, because the Scottish course at present is designed for the so-called 'least able'. Our course works for the development of such skills for every single student. We are pleased that the objectives of our course are realised by our pupils to the varying degrees of their individual potentialities within the available time-scale. They do become more skilled in listening and talking, and approaching problems constructively. They do develop more confidence in and knowledge of themselves. Their transition from school to work and society is eased. Most of all, their selfishness is reduced and they become more aware of others' needs, particularly those with special needs – and of how to help others. The pupils themselves have consistently voted the course a success, and their yearly anonymous evaluations of it will help us to try continually to improve it.

The following typical series of opinions was gathered anonymously from pupils in 1982. This quotation is typical of the tiny proportion who were against the course:

> 'I don't think that community studies is a good subject. The community placement idea is good, but when I was out I hated it. The old people I went to visit didn't want to know me. I thought they were supposed to be asked if they wanted to be visited.
>
> 'Work experience was a different story. It was good experience and I enjoyed it, even though I didn't get paid.
>
> 'What is the point of giving us sheets on smoking and Tristan de Cuna? If anyone wants to smoke, they know the consequences and can take the chance. It's a million to one against me or anyone in Westhill go to Tristan.
>
> 'Imagine making a CSE subject compulsory.'

The next represents another tiny proportion who would like the course reduced:

> 'Community studies is a useful subject as it gives you an idea of what it is like to work, but I think it should only last for the first half of the morning because a lot of the time is wasted by talking, etc. When we get taught on subjects like the blind, disabled, drugs, etc. we should get to go to more places where we can see the problems of these people and then maybe we would understand them.
>
> 'I think that community studies should be split into two halves: the first half until break should be devoted to the community studies subjects, and in the second half we should get time to study the other subjects as they are more important. With nine other subjects in the week half an hour each morning is not enough time to learn, so if we got more study time with a teacher to guide us in all of the subjects if we got into difficulty because there is no one to help us at any other time.'

The vast majority were strong in their support and constructive in their criticism, as reflected by the following example:

'I think strongly that community studies is very helpful. I felt that I could be trusted, which I felt was good. When we had to go for our job experience, it was great and it lets you understand about the job, what its like, how you work, and about yourself. And the teacher is important. Mr is a good teacher: he's not strict in certain ways (but) he knows how to handle us.'

We are perfectly well aware, of course, that the minority opinions might be the correct ones; but that so many were in favour of the continuance of the course, albeit with improvements asked for, is much more persuasive. In addition, we found a few individual opinions worthy of note:

'I think job-experience is magic I am really thrilled with it. It was the best thing that happened all my life.' (This was the entire response of this pupil.)
'During class I would like to just work at my own pace and be able to do more things for myself instead of working with the class all the time.'
'The only thing I dislike is when the teacher talks on and on: this becomes boring and I lose interest. Once said is enough . . . talk and explanation takes twenty minutes and one and a half pages have to be written in ten minutes.'
'I don't think a CSE certificate is useful in the least for a job but the knowledge gained in some of the classes is useful.'

Not only do these quotations indicate the honesty of the pupils' replies, but also their value for us, who consult pupils too infrequently.

The staff who teach, or have taught the course, have pleased us also. They have brought varying contributions to it and the pupils from their varied disciplines and experiences, as we had hoped they would. When I recently asked one of them (deliberately selected for the question because he had joined us after we had opened) how he would react were we to abandon the course, he replied that he would have been happy at that prospect six months before, but not now – the pupils would be losing too much. Another teacher, due to take one of these classes last session was so upset that he was going to complain to his teachers' union, yet, after sitting in with teachers taking these courses, he finished by looking forward to the work. I teach the course myself and find the work exhilarating. Recently, the staff as a whole expressed general support for our approach, so long as in-service training, resources, and job-protection in other subjects were guaranteed. Our community-workers were appalled that it could even be a consideration to close down our course, so convinced were they of its relevance and value to the pupils. Most parents have always supported the course. The RSA award has helped us to hold the minority in check. So long, however, as the majority of pupils support the course, it will continue and, with their help, improve.

# Pupil Submission for Consideration for RSA Book, 'Education for Capability': What I Think of the CSE in Community Studies, Westhill Academy.

In my opinion the Community Studies Course is designed to be a benefit in the future mainly by providing stepping stones from the children's sheltered world, across the battering waves of adolescence and finally to the big bad world of adulthood. If the course is completed successfully it will be an advantageous CSE in the very competitive race of ambitious school leavers all trying to achieve one goal – a career.

We cover several topics concerning the community including aggression, smoking and alcohol, technology, relationships, and very importantly, vocation. For all the topics we cover, we have several sources of information-quotes and poems, VCRs and film strips. We also received a talk from a blind person which was filmed and will be kept on tape so that it will not only be a great benefit to my class but also to those in the future. This talk took place as part of our study on need in the community. On this subject we also go on a community placement. There are three, which are spread over the two years of this subject and cover helping old, young or handicapped people. We are given the address of where we are going and left with the responsibility to, with a partner, find our own way there. This helps us to act more like adults because we are treated like one would treat a grown up.

To give us a taste of adult life we are given two weeks on work experience. We are allowed to choose what sort of work we would like to do and twice in the fourth year, we spend a week finding out what working is like. It is a great chance for us to see what we, quite possibly, will be doing if we manage to get the job we want. Even if we do not enjoy the actual labours we have to perform, it is still experience of work and might help us decide against choosing the job when we leave school or confirm our ideas that that is the job for us. The work experience is therefore very beneficial.

In class we have discussions which I personally enjoy participating in very much, as well as finding them very beneficial. In our discussions we are more or less left to ourselves. We can say what we, personally, think. There are no children brainwashed in this, the 'pupils' school'. I, as I'm sure many others do, gain a great sense of achievement in finally managing to persuade someone to see, and finally agree with my side of the argument. I, of course, always try to see what could be argued against what I say, and in fact, find it very beneficial just to listen to a discussion, to both sides. Usually almost everyone joins in the discussions because most people do have a strong idea of what they think, and this is brought out in discussions. Being given the chance to speak in front of an audience allows pupils to gradually build up their confidence.

*Audrey Mackie (Fourth-Year Student, Westhill Academy), September, 1983.*

# Pupil Submission for Consideration for RSA Book 'Education for Capability': What I think of the CSE Course in Community Studies, Westhill Academy

Having never heard of Community Studies until I moved to Westhill last year, I was interested to hear about what the subject set out to do.

And I found a varied selection of activities based around Westhill as a community. The activities we participate in, are for all age groups. This gives us a good, wide, outlook on certain sections of the community.

On our community placement we deal with three main groups; the young, old and handicapped. The experience and knowledge I have gained, has already given me more confidence outside school and home.

The opportunity to meet different people involved in these outings, gives us a greater understanding of different people, in their situations.

The school work involved in the course is just as valuable. In this, we get to deal with topics that are usually not included in the school curriculum. Over the past few months in community studies, I have covered several topics which are basic to life, but are otherwise ignored: for example, technology, relationships, aggression.

The other benefits from community studies is the social side of the subject. It teaches us the facts of alcohol and tobacco, etc; things which are affecting us but are often abused due to ignorance. The classwork presents two sides to issues like these and leaves us to choose between them.

I enjoy the course as it is interesting and above all useful. I think it's a vital part of school life, as a help to when we leave.

*Alexandra Reeves (Fourth-Year Student, Westhill Academy), September, 1983.*

# Dip. HE by Independent Study, North East London Polytechnic

*Ginny Eley, Course Tutor*

The Dip. HE by Independent Study at North East London Polytechnic admitted its first intake of seventy-two students in 1974. The James report in 1972, following a review of teacher training, suggested the need for a new, more flexible, two-year course of general education to be known as the Diploma of Higher Education. This was rapidly formally established, carrying mandatory grants. NELP proposed a course leading to general competence, which we now define as the ability to formulate and solve problems, work effectively in different contexts, work in collaboration with others, and work independently. The distinctive feature of the course was that it proposed a broad structure which gave the student the responsibility for proposing the content, mode, and assessment detail. The CNAA, which had as yet no formal model of a Dip. HE tentatively, for a trial period of one year, validated the course. As a result, students, particularly those over twenty-one without normal university entrance qualifications, now had an opportunity to enter higher education, plan courses directly responsive to individual needs, building on prior experiential learning; on obtaining their Dip. HE, to proceed to the third year of more traditional degree courses and importantly, to receive a manadatory grant for the course.

The course now has normal CNAA approval and has an annual intake of over 180 students. In the light of experience, procedures and practices have been modified and developed but the aims remain the same as in 1974, that is that students should be generally competent at the end. This gives rise to the specific objectives that all students should be able to formulate problems; plan, organize and implement programmes without dependence upon traditional models; monitor and readjust their work appropriately and judge the success and failure of their results, in the context of their own educational development, a relevant specialist area, and in areas outside their speciality; in collaboration with others, and on problems related to the needs of the community.

On joining the course, students undergo an intensive planning period, when they undertake a rigorous examination of their existing position in terms of knowledge, skills, experience and abilities, define their goals for after the course and set appropriate objectives; they then develop programmes to achieve these objectives. This individual course is presented as a statement, which is then negotiated with the school staff. A validation board, composed of eminent people outside the polytechnic and mainstream education, chaired since the outset by Sir Toby Weaver, oversees the process, and establishes the validity of programmes. They pay particular attention to the relevance of programmes to the intentions of the student after the Dip. HE.

The student's programme combines specialist studies, usually linked to a vocational aim, with group project work. There is also a range of workshop provision to help with common study and communication, and technical skills. In the specialist or individual work, while students may make use of elements of courses elsewhere in the polytechnic, it is more usual for them to focus on a particular area or problem and investigate this in some depth, using library resources to master relevant theories and background, and also including placements, observation, small-scale research, experiments or practical work to enable them to be able to take a critical stance and develop appropriate abilities. Each student will have tutorial help from specialist staff who may be based in any faculty of the polytechnic. For assessment, where doing is as or more important than knowing, the student negotiates an appropriate product and criteria for assessment. Two internal tutors then assess the product using the previously agreed criteria and, if appropriate, it is then subjected to the scrutiny of an external examiner. While the products are often in the form of dissertations, incorporating research findings, observations or placement reports, working models and reports, exhibitions of art and craft work, and videos are also submitted.

For the group project work, while students may work on placements outside, the normal groups work together within the school for a term on a project they have chosen, forming a new group the following term. In these groups the emphasis is on learning about the dynamics of task oriented groups, so as to be able to help future groups to work together more effectively; and on the various methods which can be used to lead to effective action. Here again the emphasis is on experiential learning. The final assessment is by a group project, 'the set situation', where certain requirements influence the difficulty of any project undertaken.

For entry to the programme, apart from the normal qualifications required for any degree course, specific provision is made for students over twenty-one without formal entry qualifications. Exceptionally a few students under twenty-one without two 'A' levels may also be admitted. In making decisions about entry, the course team adopts the criteria of likelihood to benefit, understanding of the course and motivation. We also specifically take into account the needs of our local community.

On obtaining the Dip. HE students can now propose plans for a one year BA/BSc Hons. by Independent Study (CNAA) within NELP, which enables them to build on their specialist studies. This course now admits students from elsewhere with the equivalent of two years of higher education. They have also transferred to a range of degree courses in other colleges and polytechnics, joined post-graduate diploma courses or gone straight into employment or self-employment.

It is perhaps easier to understand what this means in practice if we look at who the students are and what they actually do. The student body is extremely diverse. Most of the students are mature, the average being around twenty-eight, but some are in their fifties. The percentage of our intake from the boroughs around the Polytechnic, which traditionally have the lowest take-up rate of the country for higher education places, has steadily increased. There are equal numbers of men and women, although when we had a post Dip. HE primary BEd course at the Polytechnic the percentage of women increased. The student body includes all ethnic origins, with an increasing number whose parents came from the West Indies.

To give an idea of the scope of the course, the products for assessment presented in 1982 included the following: an ideas pack for teachers; sources of finance for industry and commerce; North Atlantic lobsters: their biology and management; solar concentrator systems: report and apparatus; communication in health care; analysis of traffic congestion, comparing Oxford and Milton Keynes; scientific aspects of horticulture; screen printed scarves and art work; effects of voluntary organizations on social services; a study of electric vehicle drive systems.

It can readily be seen that these cover a wide variety of areas, many inter-disciplinary and necessitating specialist knowledge and skills from technology, science, social sciences, arts and management.

In group work, the emphasis in the first two years is on understanding process, and students are encouraged to work on projects which widen their horizons and experience. The final assessment project must be relevant to the needs of the local community. The following subjects, drawn at random from recent years, illustrate the range, variety of products and emphasis on action: puppet theatre to present dental hygiene to local primary schools; tourism in the East End of London; Tactile mural for a blind centre; campaign to highlight danger of chemical dyes in fishing bait; publication (with Age Concern) of a guide to local facilities for the elderly; pollution of the Grand Union Canal; the use of redundant churches; prototype inexpensive seating for bus stops; job exchange scheme; Rastafarianism: an educational pack.

Case histories may help to elucidate the process better. Ian joined the course in 1976. Having left school without any qualifications, he had spent twelve years in the fire service before joining the Dip. HE. His interest lay with young people in trouble, and his proposal included a theoretical understanding of deviance, as well as a closer look at Intermediate Treatment as a method of coping with young offenders. His studies led him to join a national research project into Intermediate Treatment at Birmingham Polytechnic for a term, contributing to their final report. On completing the Dip. HE he joined a CQSW course, and is now a probation officer, intending to join the Degree by Independent Study as a part-time student.

Leigh joined the course in 1980. After leaving school with the equivalent of 'O' levels, for the next three years she had a variety of jobs, including secretarial, sales representative, and office manager. On the course her specialist project was designed to lead to running her own cottage industry, using silk screen printing. This involved mastering practical skills, a placement in creative print workshop, visiting exhibitions and finally producing her own exhibition of art work and printed materials. Her group projects included self defence classes for women; the hidden handicap of deafness and producing a video film. After the Dip. HE, Leigh continued to the Degree by Independent Study where she obtained a First. She has now, with the help of a GLC grant, bought some second-hand machinery and is self-employed printing socks and specialized plastic for television costumes, etc.

Ten years after its first intake, the Dip. HE by Independent Study is now nationally and internationally recognized. Its contribution to higher education has been acknowledged by established bodies and, as importantly, the reports back from ex-students after several years are encouraging, usually most supportive when, after Dip. HE, they transfer to more structural courses. The Education for Capability Award, in this case, gives outside support and recognition to a battle won within higher education institutions.

# Properties of Materials Alternative Syllabus, Heriot-Watt University

*John Cowan*

In 1975, I found myself very dissatisfied with the courses which I had designed for my learning resource centre. They offered my students control, if not independence, in their choice of study pace; and to some extent they offered a choice of the approach students might use in learning and problem-solving. But the content was still chosen by me, the teacher. I did nothing to nurture the ability to decide between what is worth studying and what is not – although that is perhaps the ultimate responsibility in through-life education.

I therefore planned a first-year subject which would have virtually no syllabus. I chose for this experiment an area where the writers of standard text books have followed different lines and where, by inference, there is a range of valid curricula possibilities. This subject, which we called 'properties and use of engineering materials' therefore encompassed a wide range of possible topics and was not linear in its logical relationships.

My aim was to introduce topics in audio-visual packages designed to establish the basic vocabulary and concepts in such a way that the learners would be stimulated to identify for themselves the real questions they would wish to answer and the topics they would wish to explore further. Having used my materials, the students were then left mainly on their own as far as content was concerned. My sole remaining contribution was to provide a framework in the form of a programme of *types* of activity in which they should engage, but one within which the *content* of the activities was to be chosen by the learners.

We met together once a week, as a group. Sometimes we took time to allow some or all of the members of the group to report back on what they had been doing and to discuss this, ask questions and even consider following up the points which had been raised. On other occasions we devoted our time, informally, to problems in study style which were arising, or perhaps just to overall appraisal.

This course ran for six experimental years, with groups of

between eight and eighteen students drawn from the entire first year class. The performance of students in the experimental group, both in this subject area and elsewhere, was markedly better than would have been predicted from the entrance qualifications. The volunteers ranged in ability, although few better entrants took this option; higher ranking school leavers preferred the security of a course in which the decisions are made by their teacher!

Several points about the experiment worried most of our visitors. I was often asked about the parts of the syllabus which a teacher would have chosen and which these students must have omitted. Eventually I replied in the words of one particular student whose response to that question was: 'Yes, we've missed out on a lot of things they've studied – but we've learnt how to learn for ourselves, so that doesn't worry us. And there are lots of things which we've studied in depth that they know nothing about at all.'

If education is synonymous with covering an appropriate syllabus, then this course is clearly open to criticism. But if it is about preparing people to learn for themselves and helping them to develop the appropriate abilities, then I am happy to stand by the answer which that student gave.

Another point which worried many visitors – and my colleagues – was the question of assessment. I exposed the alternative syllabus students to a paper which my colleagues considered appropriate in this first year subject, or (suddenly and without warning) to the paper given to the conventionally taught class. In either circumstance, the outcome was the same; the alternative syllabus students did better than conventionally taught students. They had gaps in their coverage, but their strength was in the depth of grasp which they showed in the topics which they had covered. So in later years we moved gently towards self-appraisal.

In 1982, shortly after we applied to the RSA for recognition in the 'Education for Capability' scheme, my department decided to terminate an experiment which had provoked intense controversy during the six years of its life and created strongly polarized views in the staff group. The decision was taken (happily) because it was felt desirable to incorporate the main features of the alternative syllabus approach, in a major revision of our first year curricula. And so the challenge was now to explore the possibility of carrying the initiative forward in much more strength into subsequent years of our course. But that is another story!

I look back with fairly warm feelings on the alternative syllabus course – which was my inappropriate title for a course in which I tried to have no syllabus. It was an experiment in which I made many mistakes, and one in which the students were never given as much opportunity for independence as I might now wish. But it was a time in which I glimpsed what students can achieve, even in their first year of an undergraduate course, in a context which offers them the opportunity to make real decisions and live with them. It was an experience in which I saw many young people grow up and learn to do without their teachers, and to question authority in a rigorous and constructive way. And it was an exciting time, in which I learnt that even an old authoritarian like me can be taught new tricks.

These, of course, are *my* views, but I have circulated them amongst some of the group in the final year of the experiment, inviting them to add their own (unedited) comments.

**Comments from Students in the Final Group**

Its principles – you work on a subject you're interested in and want
          to learn;
      – you work when you want to.
The benefits of this are plain to see.

*Keith Wallace*

The experience the course allowed me to gain, in working on my own or in a small group, gave me the confidence to air my own thoughts and to try my own ideas in more lines of work than were covered by the alternative syllabus course. I also feel that the course over-fulfilled its promise to the student, giving a much broader basis on the properties of materials.

*Graeme Lang*

I found the method of study employed in the alternative course beneficial not only to this course – but to the other courses studied in the first year.

*Alex Macleod*

The different teaching/learning style made the course much more interesting when set alongside the conventional – lecture, tutorial style. This meant that the students were much more happy to learn. The independence of learning meant the student was free to learn at his own rate and on subject matter chosen by himself. This responsibility for your own course of study helped the student mature more readily and developed an inquiring, engineering mind.

*Andy McLeod*

In my opinion the system achieved its basic objectives not only by asking the new undergraduate to relate himself to the construction industry via site visits, tape-slide presentations and general coursework but by building self confidence. The fact that you can be left alone to teach yourself in whatever manner, means that the person is given responsibility over course input and eventually output. From the mistakes that we made and we corrected I feel that a decided benefit is that we can realistically self-criticize our work.

*Russell Blackhall*

Choosing your topic, then learning it and teaching other students how you understood it, is, in my opinion, a simple and enjoyable way of learning. Who understands better the problems a student may have with a subject than a student?

*J Grant Murray*

# Personal Development Programme for Production Managers, University of Salford

*Bryan Allison, Director, Collaborative Studies Unit*

## The Programme

The personal development programme is a part-time, job-linked study opportunity designed to meet the needs of managers in production and related functions. The special nature of these needs and their impact on the programme are analysed later.

The programme is not a set course of lectures. It is a framework within which individual managers are encouraged to use the resources and guidance of the University to support their own development efforts. The emphasis is on helping managers to develop ability, as well as to acquire knowledge. In particular, it seeks to help them to improve their understanding of the nature, problems and methods of production management, their effectiveness in managing on-going production activities and their ability to promote and manage new industrial developments.

The programme has three inter-linked strands; problem analysis, background studies and group seminars. A manager joining the programme spends several sessions with a tutor analysing his own educational background and experience, his present job content and needs, his management style and his long-term development needs. The manager, his company and the tutor can then plan an overall development programme. This stage can also lead to immediate performance improvements and create the time which the manager needs for his own development. Suitable problems from within the manager's responsibilities are then selected for deeper study and are used as a focus for the broader examination of management subjects and methods. Progressively more complex problems are used. Tutors work with managers in their factories, as well as in the University and participants are expected to seek real, determinable performance improvements as part of the personal development process.

Background subjects and techniques are covered in tutorials and in guided personal study. Managers can also attend selected elements of formal taught courses elsewhere in the University. The sequence of personal study is determined largely by individual needs and by the problems arising in the job improvement studies. Many managers, of course, have already followed formal studies in some background subjects and techniques but often this has been isolated from practice. They frequently need help with interpretation and application rather than sitting through complete courses.

Group seminars cover special topics and contemporary developments of importance to all production managers. They also provide opportunities for participants to share the analysis of common problems, to test their ideas among peers and to make their own specialist knowledge available to the group. The value of this has been enhanced by inter-company visits. Seminar discussions range from brief reports to thorough analysis of particular real problems over several sessions. No 'artificial' case studies are used. The seminar programme is determined largely by the members of the group themselves. Participants from other programmes in the University, for example, the Teaching Company Schemes for engineers, and invited guests from industry join the group for selected sessions. Members of the programme can register for a formal qualification but few consider this important. The aim of the programme is to improve management ability, not simply to add to qualifications. Individual progress is monitored by review meetings with participants and their companies. The progress of the scheme as a whole is reviewed similarly and is guided by a steering group with industrial representation.

**Programme Development**

The personal development programme stemmed from lengthy discussions with industry during the 1970s about the general difficulties of providing educational support for production management. Production managers come from varied backgrounds and work under difficult time pressures. They need studies which are flexible in both content and method and which emphasize application and job performance, rather than simply the acquisition of subject knowledge alone. Formally taught courses are often inappropriate to their needs.

The University set up the Collaborative Studies Unit in 1979 with a very free hand to develop suitable educational facilities. The Unit was partly financed by industry and worked with a pilot group of managers and companies. Interest in the work was heightened by a number of public reports commenting on the problems of British manufacturing industry and the difficulties faced in harnessing the necessary level of production management skills. These reports particularly highlighted the need to shift management emphasis from 'fire-fighting' to long-term progress.

From a pilot group of six participants, the number on the programme has now grown to twenty from nine companies and is increasing. The structure has enabled managers of very different backgrounds to work together productively as well as developing at their own pace. Ages range from mid-twenties to mid-fifties and job responsibilities from assistant manager to divisional director. Prior educational qualifications range from nil to Phd and cover science, engineering and social sciences.

In developing the programme the Unit has drawn on some other activities in the University. These include parts of MSc courses, short courses and joint academic/practitioner study groups. Some new activities developed to support the programme have also been opened to others. The Unit now has three academic staff itself and draws help from other tutors from elsewhere in the University and industry.

### Evaluation

An important practical value of the programme is its ability to fit the time constraints of managers subject to shift working and unpredictable, urgent work demands. Necessary time away from work is minimized and the early parts of the programme help to improve time management. The flexibility also helps to cope with geographical mobility. Although a programme is normally for two years, benefits are progressive and shorter or longer periods are practicable. A limited number of participants can also be accommodated from distant factories. Some managers have modified their programme to prepare for a specific change of responsibilities.

An important educational value stems from the close integration of academic support and works application. Participants have reported an understanding of intellectual analysis and its relevance which they had not been able to achieve by more conventional (though conventionally successful) academic study. Some have valued particularly the emphasis placed on proper definition and structuring of problems and on the creative search for solutions, rather than the more common emphasis on technical aspects of problem solving.

Managers have put considerable effort into preparing material for group discussions and companies have been very open with sensitive information. Problem analysis has been thorough and honest with managers expressing growing respect for the efforts of fellow members and for the value of the process. Valuable exchanges have developed outside the formal structure. Wide differences in educational background have posed little barrier to this activity but the group itself has proved very critical of any lack of effort by participants.

The use of the manager's own job as the main study base had reduced the common problem of transferring course-learned material back to the work place. This has been further helped by bringing the manager's colleagues into discussions on an ad hoc basis where useful. Success on the programme has depended, of course, on the fact that participants and their companies are committed to real performance improvements in both the short and long term. In instances where this commitment has been weak, the value of the programme has been greatly reduced.

The programme also requires heavy commitment by tutors who must be able to work in problem terms across traditional subject boundaries. They must also be able to devise and implement new educational methods and techniques as needed in a programme which still has many problems of its own to solve. Suitable tutors are still scarce. Those who undertake the work, however, can find an integration of teaching, subject development and application with satisfactions which are difficult to match in other approaches.

The principles of the programme have proved attractive to industry. Even so, newcomers have found difficulty in appreciating the full range of opportunities available. To ensure that the implications are fully understood, all new participants start on a trial basis. This has led to firm commitment in all cases so far. User satisfaction is further demonstrated by the growing number of requests for additional work, including possibilities of extending the approach to managers in other functions. The scheme has already been extended to cover managers in works engineering. A scheme for other functions would differ in some important details. The basic principles of relating study to application, of tailoring studies to individual needs and of actively using the experience of participants in the learning process, however, are transferable. Initial work also suggests that, in the long run, the approach can be applied as economically as more standardized taught courses.

# Project Fullemploy, Clerkenwell

### Description of the Course

Project Fullemploy Clerkenwell has been offering self-employment courses to help young people to set up and run their own businesses. They are specifically aimed at non-academic people aged nineteen to twenty-five: the only kind of qualification we ask for is a skill that is well enough developed to be used for self-employment or an idea for the provision of a service. The courses run for twenty weeks making a steady progression from theoretical to practical work. Practical work is the actual running of a business: at the start of the course this takes up one day a week and towards the end it becomes the full-time activity. Course topics come under eight main headings:

Product Development: professional standards, professional advice, marketability, sample production.

Market Research: defining the market, market demand, questionnaires, surveys, testing the market.

Marketing: methods of advertising, media coverage, leaflets, business cards, catalogues, mail order, cold selling.

Self-Presentation: contacting people, making conversation, using the telephone, negotiating, time-keeping, talking to people in authority, writing letters, self-evaluation, interviewing skills.

Premises and Equipment: type of premises, facilities and location for premises, government grants, planning permission, health and safety, fire regulations, finding suppliers, using magazines and reference publications.

Finance: budgeting, overheads, cash-flow and forecast, costings, profit and loss account, balance sheet, sources of funding.

Book-keeping: petty cash book, cash book, invoicing, delivery notes, receipts, statements, banking.

Law: inland revenue, national insurance, Trades Description Act, VAT, business formats.

There are three teaching staff to an average of sixteen students. The teaching is supplemented by visits from outside speakers and business consultants who advertise on specialist areas such as VAT and insurance. Each student prepares a Business Proposal for discussion with a representative from a local bank. This forms the basis of a 'mock interview' in preparation for real-life appointments with their own bank managers. Students who have been on the course have set up a wide variety of businesses, including fashion design and manufacture, photography, hairdressing, sound and video recording, portrait painting, an errands and delivery service, woodwork and upholstery.

**The Problems the Course was Intended to Solve**

The project was set up to offer an alternative to unemployment to enterprising young people who were not being served by existing business courses. At the time all of these insisted on a high level of academic achievement – we, on the other hand, accept only unqualified people. Most of our students have either taught themselves their own skills or learnt them on other government sponsored courses.

A long-term objective is that, by enabling people to set up in business they might eventually be in the position to take on employees themselves, thus providing positive action against unemployment.

**Our Experience of Working on the Course**

An important feature of our teaching methods has been the flexibility in our approach. This begins at the interview stage. Quite often students will be very committed to the idea of self-employment but less clear as to the best use to make of their skills – by discussing their ideas with them we are often able to help to bring a focus to the different possibilities that they have been considering. As the course progresses we are always prepared for students to change direction if the need to do so becomes apparent. This is a process that can be expected and should be encouraged as developing a business also involves personal development: it therefore makes sense to keep pace with the different changes that are taking place. On one course two students began by wanting to start an accommodation service but as the problems that this involved became apparent they gradually changed direction, and are now running a successful errand and delivery service. The course runs on a tutor system – each student has a personal tutor who is responsible for monitoring progress and attending to specific needs. This personal supervision is felt to be very beneficial to the students although it can create difficulties in the amount of work that tutors are faced with. By running a course where sixteen businesses are being set up in twenty weeks tutors are often in the position of having to assimilate information about all sorts of different skills in a very short space of time so that they can be of maximum use. The demands on staff are constant so although this form of teaching is stimulating and rewarding, it can also be exhausting.

### Estimate of the Outcome of the Project

There have now been five self-employment courses and about 60 per cent of our students continue in self-employment. We feel that those who are no longer self-employed still derived benefit from the course by learning more about themselves and the types of activities that suit them, thus gaining confidence to deal with their future occupations. There have been various reasons why some students have not continued to run their own businesses. Some have lacked the necessary motivation to keep their work progressing, usually as a result of discovering that self-employment was not the right choice for them. One notable case is of a student who set up a successful bike repair business who was then persuaded by his family to give it up and enter the family french polishing business instead. The reason given was that they wanted him to have something steady behind him. This is interesting because it reflects a more widely held belief that self-employment is not really a viable option. There is an unnecessary mystique surrounding self-employment with the idea that it is somehow inaccessible. Because of this we have experienced some difficulty in recruiting people onto the course. As the course, and its success rate, become more widely publicized recruitment has become easier but we still have the task of convincing the referral agencies – such as careers offices, job centres, youth clubs – that self-employment is a viable option for young people. Once their own attitudes begin to change it can be hoped that more positive encouragement will be given to young people to choose to work for themselves.

# The Crosskeys Islwyn Challenge

*Jennifer Rowe, Noel Warkins and Susan Sims*

The Crosskeys Islwyn Challenge is in Cwmfelinfach which is in the Sirhowy Valley. It is about fifteen miles from Cardiff and in an industrial unit on an industrial estate.

The unit accommodates not only the Crosskeys Islwyn Challenge but also off-the-job trainees from the Islwyn Borough Council scheme. These trainees spend only two days a week at the unit where they mostly do construction; the other three days of the week are spent on council sites, building walls and fences.

Traditional industry in this area has always relied on coal and steel for its employment. However, over the last twenty years many pits have been closed and the work force in the steel plants at Ebbw Vale, Port Talbot and Llanwern has been dramatically reduced. Job prospects in the coal and steel industries now no longer exist, but it has been anticipated that over the next twenty years industry in South Wales will be based on small units employing twenty to 200 people and covering a wide range of manufacturing and service industries.

All trainees at the Challenge are aged between sixteen and eighteen and, because the boys and girls work together in mixed groups, the ratio at the Challenge as a whole is 50:50. Trainees are at different levels of education. Some trainees have problems with reading and writing whereas others have obtained some 'O' levels or even one or two 'A' levels.

The Challenge is supported by the local education authority, the Crosskeys Tertiary College, Islwyn Borough Council and the Manpower Services Commission. The Challenge itself is named after the famous poet, Islwyn, who is buried in a small chapel only a few hundred yards away from our unit.

It is possible for trainees to follow a variety of vocational routes. Each route starts with the basic principles and progresses to more complex techniques.

The 'construction route' is made up of several different areas: building, painting, decorating and carpentry. Within this route the trainees built the seminar rooms, the canteen and the dark room. They then fitted the windows and doors and painted the interiors.

The next route is 'engineering and the motor vehicle'. In this route the trainees are taught to maintain and service a motor car. They are also taught how to use a bending machine, a lathe, an oxy-acetylene welder and an arc welder. With these skills they have built a kit car which they call 'The Hustler'.

Another route is 'child care and social welfare'. During their time in this route the trainees learn how to deal with young children, especially babies. They are taught how to change babies' nappies, how to bathe the baby and also how to sterilize the equipment to be used.

The fourth route is 'catering'. This is split into two separate areas. The first is the provision of a canteen service to trainees, staff and workers from other factories on the estate, and for this they supply a varied and changing menu. The second area is the learning of basic kitchen skills such as following recipes, using machinery and cleaning the kitchen.

The last route is 'office and clerical'. In this route the trainees run the factory by sending out letters, checking goods in and out and filing in-coming information. As well as this, the trainees are taught office skills such as typing and using the telephone switchboard.

In addition to these five main routes there is also a 'support route' which is printing and photography.

There is no sex stereotyping: all trainees are encouraged to do all the routes. The girls are encouraged to do construction and carpentry and the boys are encouraged to work in the canteen.

As well as the routes there is also a compulsory section called 'core studies'. In this, the trainees get social and life skills, basic numeracy and literacy and also computing, using the computer we have in the office.

Organization and structure of the Challenge includes eight important elements. It is a forty-eight week period, involving eight weeks actually on site and eight weeks out on placement, and this pattern is repeated throughout the course.

There is a production element, which currently involves equipment for playgroups. Revenue from this source finances expeditions and the purchasing of equipment.

Another element is residential: we take two sessions each of two weeks, mainly outdoor activities; for example, canoeing and rock climbing.

Next comes job search. Throughout the course, and really from the first day, the trainee is encouraged to look for a permanent job by taking interviews wherever possible. Last year we had a 60 per cent record of trainees actually getting permanent jobs by the end of the course.

There is a negotiated timetable. It provides trainees with a multi-skill background. First, they choose a main vocational route and then follow a balanced timetable. Each day is divided into two sessions, morning and afternoon, thus making ten sessions in all in a five-day week. Within these ten sessions, five are for the main vocational route, two are the computer and core, leaving three sessions with one or more secondary route.

We also have guidance and counselling. Each trainee is allocated to his or her personal tutor. Guidance and counselling takes place at least once a fortnight and any problems that may arise can then be sorted out.

Finally, assessment is of a continuous nature. At the end of every three-hour session the trainees are asked to make a self-assessment. On these assessment sheets the task or activity is broken down into a series of steps and within these steps, six in all, the trainees make a self-assessment varying from 'very easy' to 'very difficult'. With the aid of these assessments, log books or diaries can be kept. The trainees can write comments on the course as well as their own performance.

Of course, the Challenge has had its problems. All trainees are at different educational levels, so it is necessary for lecturers to sub-divide tasks very carefully so that each trainee can gain satisfaction from achieving real objectives. This also requires lecturers to have an intimate knowledge of the educational capability of each trainee.

This is conducted in a classroom split into several sections. Because it is conducted in a classroom many of the trainees resent this as it is too much like a school atmosphere. To remedy this problem, core studies are conducted during the job they are participating in.

Another problem is that of diminishing numbers, since 60 per cent of trainees may leave to take permanent jobs.

# CHAPTER 13
# Towards Capability
*Fred Flower*

In the five years since the publication of the manifesto and its endorsement by some 250 public figures, the campaign for Education for Capability has registered a number of successes. It has singled out seventy-one examples among over 300 submissions and given them public recognition as expressions of education for capability. It has effectively propagated the concept of Capability, by article and lecture, so that very many people have heard of it and would recognize it as a good thing, even if it is a rather smaller number who understand it and wish to see it effective in practice. In spite of this initial success it has not so far succeeded in deflecting the education system from what many perceive as its main purpose, maximizing the number of pupils and students obtaining academic qualifications, or in modifying most of its long established practices designed to achieve that limited goal. Unlike the Walls of Jericho, bastions of the system are unlikely to fall to the blasts of trumpets, even such well-tempered and effective instruments as may be blown by the Royal Society of Arts.

In weighing up what still has to be accomplished, it is easy to underestimate the real achievements of the campaign to date. A new phase was ushered in with the appointment of a Fellow and a Consultant in October 1983 and the first task they set themselves was to survey the projects that had been recognized and discover what the effect of recognition had been. The results of the survey have proved pleasantly encouraging. Forty-three questionnaires were sent out, covering the projects in 1980, 1981 and 1982; 33 were returned completed, two sent letters and seven who had had some difficulty in completing made full responses to telephone inquiries. Thus a fairly detailed picture emerged of how recognition had affected these projects. All but two of them were still functioning, most of them going from strength to strength. The first of the lapsed projects was a part-time postgraduate course in Design and Manufacture at Heriot-Watt University that had exhausted its immediate local market. The University hoped to revive it in the 1985–86 session. The other was an industrial project – the schools liaison work of Metal Box – and this had been very much the concern of one person who had now left. Two projects were threatened through a loss of resources but all the remaining thirty-nine were continuing to flourish and in many cases to develop.

In the responses to specific questions, 80 per cent of respondents believed they had influenced developments within their institutions and 45 per cent other local developments, while some 41 per cent believed that they had had some influence on national developments. Only one of the forty-three thought that the effect of recognition was marginal: 'RSA recogniton', they wrote, 'was warmly appreciated by all involved but it has not been a major factor in obtaining recogniton of the course's virtues either internally or externally.' This did not reflect the experience of other institutions. Far more typical was the comment: 'Recognition had made staff realize we are doing something worthwhile and given us help in attracting students and influencing outside validation bodies.' The three elements noted here: the enhancement of self-esteem among the project staff, the publicity value of recognition, and its use as a support (or, on occasion, a defence) in dealing with external bodies – CNAA, NAB, HM Inspectorate or even the LEA – were mentioned again and again. Among the most important effects of recognition has been the convincing of the staff engaged in these projects that they were not operating in isolation in a hostile and unappreciative world. It helped to change the perception of 'influential and senior personnel with very traditional views on pedagogy' in one institution and 'unaware, hostile staff' in another. Above all, it helped to convince pupils of the 'validity of their work.' As another respondent said, it acted as a 'valid form of external evaluation', and this referred to the work of a primary school where such evaluation is hard to come by. At the other end of the spectrum, a university don wrote: 'More importantly, the RSA recognition gave credibility to an innovative programme of study.

This credibility has been immensely helpful to us both within the university and outside. In retrospect, there is no doubt the visit . . . both drew our attention to and helped us to clarify our minds on a number of issues concerning the long-term development of our activities. At the time of their visit we did not fully appreciate how helpful their fresh and probing comments on our work had been.'

Three further statements indicated how some institutions perceived recognition as a major step forward: 'The accession of a powerful and respected voice in the campaign for Education for Capability is the most important breakthrough for us since 1967' was the comment of a well known pioneer in the development of personal records of school children. Another school that had quite a struggle to win acceptance for its community studies programme (common to the whole age group) was convinced that RSA recognition had 'improved the public status of the school in its general attempt to change the way pupils are treated, what they are taught, how they are taught, how examined and how consulted.' One of the most heartwarming effects of recognition was upon a university course in which recognition 'prompted a totally new staff-student initiative in a different, more challenging, more worthwhile area. This has been a splendid outcome *directly* of the presentation meeting last year.'

And yet the very success of the campaign so far may prove to be a hindrance to its further advance. The appeal of Capability is such that it has been able to bring together at the four symposia at which presentations have been made, representatives of a wide spectrum of educational opinion including many who would find it difficult to agree in another forum. This at once prompts the question, does 'capability' mean the same to each one of those present? It has hitherto been the fate of an educational notion when it has become common currency so that it no longer requires definition, to lose shape and precision and finally vanish as a cliché in a puff of wind. A fashionable term is made to serve each user's own purposes which may be far from those of the original coiners. Such practices help forward the process by which the education system appears to adapt to changing circumstance by recognizing innovative practice, but in fact simply absorbs it without major change. Any apparent effect is likely to be short lived or fairly cosmetic, for the inertia of the system is formidable. Anything that threatens to disturb its equilibrium is swiftly neutralized not by any conspiracy of those working within it but by the simple operation of its normal curricular processes. For many, this impressive stability no doubt appears as a virtue of the system. They will regard its relative imperviousness to major change as a safeguard to standards and achievement. On the other hand, the volume of criticism of the irrelevance of much of what happens to people within education and to their needs and aspirations bears testimony of quite a different order. The disenchantment of many young people and adults with their experience of formalized learning and the growing frustration of an expanding number of teachers suggests the necessity for major change.

A term widely used on the assumption that it now has a meaning commonly accepted, may find its value slowly diluted until its use in some contexts may totally negate the meaning its originators had intended. Is such a fate in store for Education for Capability? The recognition award is itself a means of helping to ensure that this dilution does not take place. The Committee, by refining its statement of the aims of Education for Capability and spelling out more precisely the criteria it uses for its assessment, has taken steps to safeguard the interpretation embodied in the manifesto.

Three dangers, even so, threaten a wider adoption and application of the concepts. It may be reduced to a feature worthy in its own right but mainly manifested in activities marginal to the main activity of the educational institution. Alternatively, it may exist in parallel with, but without any organic relation to, what are perceived as the major elements of the curriculum much in the same way as 'general studies' or 'liberal studies' have tended to do in the past. Or in the third case it may through circumstance come to be attached to low status activities within the curriculum and thus itself come to be considered a low status activity inappropriate for inclusion in the timetable of those pursuing mainly academic studies. Even within the range of projects already recognized one is aware of the existence of these dangers. Valuable as the projects have proved as models and while most embrace a whole course or a whole group, a recognized project has rarely involved the whole institution. Where it has, it has usually been untypical of mainstream education: a highly specialized agency, a non-traditional degree course, a primary school, an unorthodox school from the private sector or a vocational preparation scheme. It is not to be expected that it would happen otherwise. It is always easier to innovate in a new development rather than in the main bread and butter areas of activity. But the very fact that such new developments are the cradles of development of Capability can threaten to keep it at the margins, or merely in parallel or confined to low status activity such as vocational preparation.

The irony is that as the authors of the manifesto and those who endorsed it have recognized, Education for Capability is a feature that needs to be incorporated into the very heart of educational practice and the traditional academic courses neglect it at their peril. The need for major change is widely recognized today but in spite of a many sided debate and the many separate initiatives of a variety of individuals and institutions the inertia within the system has hitherto acted as an effective brake on progress. The system of public examinations has been widely identified as a major obstacle to change and yet years, even decades, of debate have failed to find ways of replacing it or even effectively modifying it. A second obstacle depending on the first has been the organization and hierarchical administrative structure of schools and colleges so that the personal expectations and career prospects of teachers get meshed in with the imperatives laid upon the institution by the system of examinations. Finally, the third obstacle has been the success of the system in selling itself so that the expectations of parents, employers, and of the students and pupils themselves are initially structured in terms of examination success though the real outcomes they all seek have ultimately nothing to do with examinations.

The solution to the dilemma is easy to posit. A 'capability curriculum' in which all the activities undertaken by the learner operate in harmony to produce in each person to a greater or lesser degree the four capacities identified by the award scheme:

'They want to improve their *competence* by the practice of skills and the use of knowledge; to *cope* better with their own lives and the problems that confront them and society; to develop their *creative* abilities and, above all, to *co-operate* with other people.'

It is, however, far easier to outline what a 'capability

curriculum' would look like and how it would function in a Utopia than to take the first steps towards initiating it. Three or four strategies present themselves. The first is to continue as at present, in the hope that a sufficient number of examples of Education for Capability will accumulate to allow the system's inertia to be overcome and a general, if piecemeal, reform will take place. Secondly, there could be a major frontal assault on the system of public examinations on the grounds that it is the main blockage on the route to change. As the experience of the relatively minor assaults of the last two decades reveal, such a battle in its ineffectual waste of time and resources would summon up images of the Hindenberg Line or Passchendaele. An alternative strategy already favoured by some is for fresh objectives to be set for the education system for some not too distant date – twenty years' time, for example – and for the experts to convince the establishment of the rightness of their thinking and then to impose from above the frame that will produce the necessary changes. This is a strategy that has much to commend it but unless it is decked out with meretricious trappings is unlikely to catch and inspire the imagination of those at the grass roots – teachers and learners – whose willing consent and co-operation is the essential ingredient of any formula for success.

A body like the Royal Society of Arts seeking to promote a 'capability curriculum' is then left with only one line of strategy. It needs to be a natural growth out of its own tradition and out of what has already been accomplished in the last four years. To continue the military metaphor, in contrast to frontal assault of grand design, a guerilla strategy is to be preferred. A carefully co-ordinated and sustained campaign of individual action within a gradually developing frame of action undermines or by-passes the blocks, weakens support for them and wins hearts and minds by demonstrating the superiority of the educational practice it promotes.

The Recognition Scheme must continue to be the base from which the campaign for Education for Capability sets out. It cannot, however, avoid developing and changing as the campaign proceeds. The Committee has invited those who intend to make submissions to consult with the society staff beforehand should they wish; so that they can be sure their thinking is consonant with the Committee's. We may be able to extend and share the experience of others with them and perhaps broaden the scope of their original concept.

Up to 1983 the Recognition Scheme singled out good practice and the Symposium called public attention to it. The further stage of the campaign that opened in that year has tackled the task of dissemination of the Education for Capability message on a more extended scale. Based on the examples that have already come to light through the Recognition Scheme a data bank and information exchange is evolving. As in other aspects of the campaign the Society cannot work in isolation or in competition. As it develops its own information network it must be able to plug into other networks that are prepared to give and receive information on a reciprocal basis. Thus the Education for Capability Committee looks to consolidate the links it has already established with the Centre for the Study of Comprehensive Schools, the Council for Educational Technology and several similar bodies, a number of local education authorities and certain major industrial and commercial undertakings.

Storing and exchanging information may be the first step towards disseminating the capability message, but ultimate success will require the campaign to undertake more promotional activity. Two channels readily available are through publications – its own and other peoples' – and through conferences and working groups.

Since March 1984 a regular Newsletter has been published each term. It reports developments in the field and other items of current interest. Each issue, in addition, explores a facet of Education for Capability by means of short articles commissioned from expert contributors. Assessment, Vocational Education and Continuity between the stages and levels of Education and Training have been themes for recent issues. A fuller treatment of Education for Capability themes is reserved for the Occasional Papers published irregularly two or three times a year that have so far examined aspects of assessment, school organization, independent learning and the training of professionals. Occasional Papers have included specially commissioned pieces and also accounts of work important for the further development of education for capability but which may not in themselves be appropriate for consideration for recognition.

Activity through conferences and workshops is the other main line of development. The Society has participated in conferences organized by others either by supplying speakers or organizing a workshop. It has also organized its own conferences nationally and regionally.

The first major conference of the campaign 'Opportunities and Obstacles' was held during the autumn of 1984 and the spring of 1985. Arranged in co-operation with the Centre for the Study of Comprehensive Schools it took place on two days, four months apart: this allowed the activity of the first day to provide material for the second. Participants were invited to use their experience to identify the problems of practice and possible solutions. Based on case studies, the first day was concerned to frame questions which were presented on the second day to a panel of people in a position to facilitate change by removing or mitigating some of the obstacles. A follow-up to the conference is concerned with the further elaboration of strategies for change and priorities for action.

A good example of a regional conference (and of the co-operative mode of presentation) was that held in November 1984 and organized jointly by the Society, Brathay Hall Trust and Cumbria LEA, with a contribution from the Grubb Institute. The theme of the conference was the personal and social development of young people and how they may find a provision to meet their needs, among the maze of educational and training schemes at present on offer to the fourteen to nineteen age group. The audience was drawn from those involved with this age group in school, college, youth service, and youth training schemes.

At this stage of the campaign there was a significant emphasis on the secondary school and the immediate post secondary phase but in the wake of the national conference the focus has shifted on to continuity in education for capability, and how the secondary experience can tie in with that of both higher and continuing education as well as with that of the primary school. Activity on a regional basis is being stimulated, and while it is primarily concerned with those problems that are of most immediate interest to the local participants will, it is hoped, encourage the exchange of experience and the lessons of practice between the major sectors of education.

The Capability Curriculum that will steadily emerge over the next few years we should expect not only to give expression to the four elements of competence, coping, creativity and co-operative action, but to do so in ways that would include a measure of learner control over what he or she is learning through negotiation, independent learning systems and experiential learning. If such activity is to be a central part of Education for Capability cognizance must be taken of it in the forms of assessment used. The Framework for Initiatives has already been discussed and is an essential and rational component of the campaign. But just as the campaign would be quite unable to present one preferred solution to all the problems thrown up by the many alternative forms of a 'capability curriculum', there cannot at this stage be a single or orthodox solution to the problems of assessment. In this field as in the matter of curriculum itself, Education for Capability adopts a co-operative, not a competitive, stance and welcomes such intiatives as the DES policy statement on records of achievement or Sir Keith Joseph's proposals to the North of England Conference in January 1984.

It is not only with the forms of assessment that Education for Capability is concerned, but also with the use to which they are subsequently put. Although the pattern of traditional examinations·may be faulted on technical grounds, for example, norm referencing rather than criterion referencing, the real objections to the system stem from its inappropriate use as an instrument for selection for employment or entry into higher education and the consequent pressure this exerts on the schools. It may be more fruitful to discuss alternative forms of selection which may prove more effective in the long run with employers and higher education institutions than wasting a lot of time in attempting to improve what are widely recognized as impotent instruments. To quote Professor Handy again: 'There is a view of the process of change which says that it is often as effective to remove or dismantle the blocks to change as it is to build up the forces for change. Remove the blocks and the repressed energies surge forth.'

It was this thought that dictated the choice of topic for Education for Capability's first national conference 'Opportunities and Obstacles' and prompted the particular format in which those people who might be held to represent some of the obstacles were invited to respond to the case which the earlier session of the conference had proposed.

The Recognition Scheme, information and dissemination, and

new forms of assessment are three main lines of advance for the campaign at the present stage. A fourth might be some form of active research investigating the precise nature of a Capability Curriculum and the mode or modes of establishing it. Co-operation between the RSA, an LEA, an industrial sponsor and bodies representing both schools and further education might establish a firm basis for such a piece of work.

Such is the outline of the activity envisaged in the next stage of the campaign for Education for Capability. It has taken six years to reach this point. The gathering momentum of the campaign and the growing volume of support for the kind of thinking that infuses it suggest that third milestone will be reached in a much shorter time.

# Appendix 1

**The Signatories to the Manifesto**

(The signatories were asked to support the Manifesto as individuals and not on behalf of any particular organization)

| | |
|---|---|
| Elizabeth Adams | Editor, *Journal of the National Association of Inspectors & Educational Advisers* |
| Kenneth Adams CVO | Comino Fellow, Royal Society of Arts; Associate Fellow, St George's House, Windsor Castle |
| Sir Campbell Adamson | Chairman, Abbey National Building Society |
| Robert Aitken | Director of Education, Coventry |
| Lord Alexander | formerly General Secretary, Association of Education Committees |
| Lindsay Anderson | Film and Theatre Director |
| Stuart Andrews | Headmaster, Clifton College, Bristol; Editor, Journal of the Headmasters' Conference |
| Peter E. Andry | Director, International Classical Division, EMI Music |
| M.A. Anson | Director, National Westminster Bank |
| Professor Bruce Archer CBE | Head, Department of Design Research, Royal College of Art |

Sir Ove Arup CBE — Founder, Ove Arup Partnership

Professor John Ashworth — Vice-Chancellor, University of Salford

Sir Richard Attenborough CBE — Chairman, British Film Institute; Deputy Chairman, Channel 4 Television

Professor the Lord Baker OBE FRS — Chairman, IDC Consultants; formerly Head of Department of Engineering, Cambridge University

Sir Peter Baldwin KCB — formerly Permanent Secretary, Department of Transport

Professor Sir James Ball — Principal, London Business School; Chairman, Legal and General Group

Correlli Barnett — Keeper of the Archives and Fellow, Churchill College, Cambridge

Sir Donald Barron DL — Chairman, Midland Bank

Stephen Bayley — Director, The Boiler House, Victoria and Albert Museum

Lord Beaumont of Whitley — Liberal spokesman on education and the arts, House of Lords

Sir Terence Beckett CBE — Director-General, CBI

C.M. Beddow — Chairman and Chief Executive, London and Midland Industrials

Eileen D. Bell — Headmistress, Helena Romanes School, Great Dunmow, Essex

| | |
|---|---|
| The Rt Hon Lord Beswick JP | formerly Chairman, British Aerospace |
| Dr David Bethel CBE | Director, Leicester Polytechnic |
| Michael Bett | Board Member for Personnel and Industrial Relations, British Telecom |
| Dr C.W.L. Bevan CBE | Vice-Chancellor, University of Wales |
| Sir Timothy Bevan | Chairman, Barclays Bank |
| Baroness Birk JP | Labour Environment Spokesman, House of Lords |
| Tom Blumenau | Managing Director, Rexgrove |
| Stephen Bragg | Regional Broker (Eastern Region), Science & Engineering Research Council |
| Heather Brigstocke | High Mistress, St Paul's Girls School, London |
| D. Brockington | Director, Youth Education Service, Bristol |
| Professor Daphne Brooker | Head of Fashion, Kingston Polytechnic |
| Sir Arthur Bryan | Chairman, Wedgwood |
| Tyrrell Burgess | Reader in the Philosophy of Social Institutions and Dean of Continuing Education, North East London Polytechnic |

Raymond Burton                      formerly Chairman, Burton
                                    Group

Sir Adrian Cadbury                  Chairman, Cadbury Schweppes

Sir Alec Cairncross KCMG FBA Chancellor, Glasgow University;
                                    formerly Economic Adviser to
                                    HM Government

The Viscount Caldecote DSC          Chairman, Investors in Industry

E. Frank Candlin OBE                Vice-President, and Chairman,
                                    Examinations Board, Royal
                                    Society of Arts

Sherban Cantacuzino                 Secretary, Royal Fine Art
                                    Commission

The Rt Hon Lord Carr                Chairman, Prudential
                                    Corporation; formerly Home
                                    Secretary

David Carter CBE RDI                Chairman and Managing
                                    Director, DCA Design
                                    Consultants; Member, Design
                                    Council

Terry Casey CBE                     Vice President,
                                    International Federation of Free
                                    Teachers Union; formerly
                                    General Secretary, National
                                    Association of Schoolmasters/
                                    Union of Women Teachers

John Cassels CB                     Director General, National
                                    Economic Development Office

Lady Casson                         Senior Fellow, Royal College of
                                    Art

| | |
|---|---|
| Sir Geoffrey Chandler CBE | Director, Industry Year 1986; formerly Director-General, National Economic Development Office |
| E.P. Chappell CBE | Director, Morgan Grenfell Holdings; Treasurer, Royal Society of Arts |
| Lord Chapple | formerly General Secretary, Electrical, Electronic, Telecommunication and Plumbing Union |
| C.V. Chester-Browne | Managing Director, Vickers Design and Projects |
| Sir Henry Chilver FRS | Vice-Chancellor, Cranfield Institute of Technology |
| Demetrius Comino OBE | President, Dexion-Comino International |
| Sir Terence Conran | Chairman, Habitat Mothercare |
| Sir Kenneth Corfield | Chairman and Chief Executive, Standard Telephones & Cables |
| Patrick Cormack MP | Member of Parliament for Staffordshire South (Conservative) |
| Peter Cox OBE | formerly Principal, Dartington College of Arts |
| The Rt Hon Lord Craigton CBE | Chairman, All-Party Conservation Committee; formerly Chairman, United Biscuits |

| | |
|---|---|
| Lord Crathorne DL | Fine Art Consultant; Director, Blakeney Hotels |
| David Crouch MP | Member of Parliament for Canterbury (Conservative) |
| Professor Sir Samuel Curren DL FRS | Visiting Professor in Energy Studies, University of Glasgow |
| Dr Duncan Davies | Chief Engineer and Scientist, Department of Industry |
| N. Olwen Davies | Headmistress, St Swithun's School, Winchester |
| Peter Dawson | General Secretary, National Association of Teachers in Further and Higher Education |
| The Rt Hon Edmund Dell | Chairman, Channel 4 Television; formerly Secretary of State for Trade |
| H.J. Dunster CB | Director, National Radiological Protection Board |
| The Rt Hon Viscount Eccles CH KCVO | Trustee, British Museum; formerly Minister of Education |
| Alan Eden-Green | Consultant, Industry and Parliament Trust |
| Sir Michael Edwardes | Executive Chairman, Dunlop Holdings |
| Professor E.G. Edwardes | formerly Vice-Chancellor and Principal, University of Bradford |
| Dr Charles Elliott | formerly Director, Christian Aid |

| | |
|---|---|
| Glyn England | formerly Chairman, Central Electricity Generating Board; Chairman, Council for Environmental Conservation |
| A.N. Fairbairn MC | formerly Director of Education, Leicestershire |
| Sebastian de Ferranti | Director, Ferranti |
| Sir Monty Finniston FRS | Chancellor, University of Stirling; Visiting Fellow, University of Lancaster |
| Jean Floud CBE | formerly Principal, Newnham College, Cambridge |
| The Lord Flowers FRS | Vice Chancellor, University of London |
| Michael Fores | Writer |
| Sir Denis Forman OBE | Chairman, Granada Television |
| Michael Forman | formerly Group Personnel Director, TI Group |
| Professor Peter Forrester CBE | Professor Emeritus, Cranfield School of Management; Consultant, Open University |
| Norman Foster | Senior Partner, Foster Associates (Architects) |
| Sir Campbell Fraser | Chairman, Scottish Television |
| Professor C. Freeman | Director, Science Policy Research Unit, University of Sussex |

| | |
|---|---|
| Dr E.A. Freeman | Director, Trent Polytechnic |
| A.F. Frodsham CBE | formerly Director-General, Engineering Employers Federation |
| Sir Peter Gadsden GBE | Underwriting Member of Lloyd's; formerly Lord Mayor of London |
| Dr Maurice Goldsmith | Director, Science Policy Foundation |
| G.T. Goodall | Headmaster, Exeter School Devonshire |
| Peter Gorb | Senior Fellow in Design Management, London Business School |
| Antoinette Gordon | Member of Council, University of Birmingham |
| S.T. Graham CBE DFC | Director, Midland Bank |
| Keith Grant | Director, Design Council |
| Roy Grantham | General Secretary, Association of Professional, Executive, Clerical and Computer Staff |
| Harry Greenway MP | Member of Parliament for Ealing North (Conservative) |
| A.H.C. Greenwood | formerly Deputy Chairman, British Aerospace |
| The Lord Gregson DL | Executive Director, Fairey Holdings |

| | |
|---|---|
| Professor Sir George Grenfell-Baines OBE DL | Founder Partner, Building Design Partnership |
| Robin Guthrie | Director, Joseph Rowntree Memorial Trust |
| General Sir John Hackett GCB CBE DSO | Author; formerly Principal, King's College, London |
| Michael Haines | Partner, Thompson McLintock Co |
| G.R. Hall | Director, Brighton Polytechnic |
| Sir Peter Hall CBE | Director, National Theatre |
| Professor Charles Handy | Visiting Professor, London Business School |
| Professor Sir Alan Harris CBE | Senior Partner, Harris and Sutherland |
| Dame Diana Reader Harris DBE | Vice-President, Royal Society of Arts; formerly Headmistress, Sherborne School for Girls |
| G.M.A. Harrison CBE | Chief Education Officer, Sheffield |
| Sir Robert Haslam | Chairman, Tate & Lyle |
| Professor John Heath | Professor of Economics, London Business School |
| R.L. Helmore CBE | Principal, Cambridgeshire College of Arts and Technology |
| Professor Peter Herriot | Head, Department of Occupational Psychology, Birbeck College, University of London |

B.J. Hill

Managing Director, Higgs and Hill

Sir John Hill FRS

formerly Chairman, British Nuclear Fuels; formerly Chairman, United Kingdom Atomic Energy Authority

Dr Graham Hills

Principal and Vice-Chancellor, University of Strathclyde

Professor F.H. Hinsley OBE

formerly Vice-Chancellor, University of Cambridge

Dr Anne Hogg

Design researcher; Member of Council, Brunel University, Girls' Public Day School Trust

Sir Christopher Hogg

Chairman and Chief Executive, Courtaulds

Geoffrey Holroyde

Director, Coventry Lanchester Polytechnic

Dr J.H. Horlock FRS

Vice-Chancellor, Open University

F.H. Howorth OBE

Chairman and Managing Director, Howorth Air Engineering Group

Professor Liam Hudson

Head, Department of Psychology, Brunel University

T.C. Hudson CBE

formerly Chairman, ICL

Sir Ian Hunter MBE

Vice-President, Royal Society of Arts; Chairman and Managing Director, Harold Holt

| | |
|---|---|
| A.C. Hutchinson JP | Principal, Paddington College |
| Professor Stanley Hutton | Head, Department of Mechanical Engineering, University of Southampton |
| Donald Insall OBE | Director, Donald Insall & Associates (Architects) |
| Jeremy Isaacs | Chief Executive, Channel 4 Television |
| Professor Elliott Jaques | Professor of Sociology and Director, Institute of Organization and Social Studies, Brunel University |
| Dick Jeeps CBE | Chairman, The Sports Council |
| Simon Jenkins | Political Editor, The Economist |
| Michael Johnson | formerly Director of Education, London Borough of Harrow |
| Dr Tom Johnston | Principal and Vice-Chancellor, Heriot-Watt University |
| Dr Hugh Jolly | Physician in charge of Paediatric Department, Charing Cross Hospital, London |
| Anne Jones | Head, Cranford Community School, Hounslow, Middlesex |
| Professor the Lord Kaldor FBA | Professor Emeritus of Economics, King's College, Cambridge |

| | |
|---|---|
| The Lord Keith of Castleacre | Vice-Chairman, Beecham Group; Non-Executive Director, Guinness Peat Aviation Group |
| Dr A.J. Kennedy CBE | Deputy Director, Technical Change Centre |
| The Rt Hon Neil Kinnock MP | Leader of the Opposition, Member of Parliament for Islwyn (Labour) |
| The Lord Kissin | President, Guinness Peat Group |
| Harry Knutton CB | Director-General, City and Guilds of London Institute |
| Sir Hans Kornberg FRS | Sir William Dunn Professor of Biochemistry, University of Cambridge |
| Sir Maurice Laing | formerly Chairman, John Laing |
| Robin Leigh-Pemberton | Governor, Bank of England |
| Professor Douglas Lewin | Professor of Electronics, University of East Anglia |
| Peter Lewis | Chairman, John Lewis Partnership |
| B.C. Lindley | Director of Technology, Dunlop |
| Sir Norman Lindop | Principal, British School of Osteopathy |
| Dr Brian B Lloyd | Chairman, Oxford Gallery and Emeritus Fellow of Magdalen College, Oxford; formerly Director, Oxford Polytechnic |

| | |
|---|---|
| W.B.H. Lord CB | Consultant |
| Owen Luder | Architect |
| Professor Tom Lupton | Director, Manchester Business School |
| John Lyons | General Secretary, Engineers and Managers Association |
| Ian MacGregor | Chairman, National Coal Board |
| The Lord Mais of Walbrook GBE TD DL JP | formerly Director, Royal Bank of Scotland |
| John Mann | Director of Education, London Borough of Harrow |
| Alistair Mant | Dean, Faculty of Administrative Studies, Polytechnic of the South Bank, London |
| Victor Margrie CBE | Director of Craft Development, Royal College of Art |
| The Lord Marshall of Leeds | Vice-Chairman, Conservative Party; Vice-President, Building Societies Association |
| Sir Peter Masefield | Deputy Chairman, Caledonian Aviation Group; Vice-President, Royal Society of Arts |
| Gerald McDonald OBE | formerly Chairman, BBC Music Advisory Committee; formerly Administrator, National Opera Studio |
| The Lord McFadzean of Kelvinside | formerly Chairman, Rolls Royce |

| | |
|---|---|
| Sir Patrick Meaney | Chairman, The Rank Organization |
| Dame Margaret Miles DBE | formerly Headmistress, Mayfield School, Putney, London |
| Sir Bernard Miller | Treasurer, Southampton University; formerly Chairman, Retail Distributors' Association |
| I.N. Momtchiloff | General Manager, Investors in Industry |
| Michael Montague CBE | Chairman, National Consumer Council; Chairman, Valor Company |
| Professor John Morris | Managing Partner, Development Consortium at the Manchester Business School |
| Sir Claus Moser KCB CBE | Vice-Chairman, N.M. Rothschild & Sons; Chairman, Economist Intelligence Unit |
| Martin Moss CBE | Director, National Trust (Enterprises); Vice-President Royal Society of Arts |
| Dr A.E. Moulton CBE | Managing Director, Moulton Developments |
| Peter Newsam | Chairman, Commission for Racial Equality |
| Sir David Nicolson | Chairman, Rothmans International |

Sir Edwin Nixon CBE

Chairman and Chief Executive, IBM UK; Chairman, Joint Board for Pre-Vocational Education

Sir Arthur Norman KBE DFC

Chairman, The De La Rue Company

Dr Patrick Nuttgens CBE

Director, Leeds Polytechnic

Sir Richard O'Brien DSO MC

Chairman, Engineering Industry Training Board; formerly Chairman, Manpower Services Commission

Orlando Oldham

Chairman, Oldham Foundation

Dame Kathleen Ollerenshaw DBE

Chairman of Court, Royal Northern College of Music; formerly Lord Mayor of Manchester

Sir David Orr MC

Chairman, Inchcape; Vice-President, Royal Society of Arts

Sir John Osborn MP

Member of Parliament for Sheffield, Hallam (Conservative)

John Osola CBE

Director, John Osola and Associates; Secretary, Fellowship of Engineering

Sir Alexander Page MBE

Chairman, Electrolux

Sir Frederick Page CBE FRS

formerly Chairman and Chief Executive, Aircraft Group, British Aerospace

Derek Palmar

Chairman and Chief Executive, Bass Group

Sir Peter Parker MVO

Chairman, Rockware Group; Chairman, British Institute of Management

Professor R.K. Penny

Head of Instrumentation, School of Engineering and Science, The Polytechnic of Central London

The Lord Perry of Walton FRS OBE

formerly Vice Chancellor, Open University

W.H. Petty CBE

County Education Officer, Kent

James Pilditch CBE

founder, AIDCOM International; Chairman, Design Board, Business and Technician Education Council

Sir Alastair Pilkington FRS

Director, Pilkington Brothers

Baroness Platt of Writtle CBE DL

Chairman, Equal Opportunities Commission

Lady Plowden DBE

formerly Chairman, Independent Broadcasting Authority; President, National Institute of Adult Education

The Lord Plowden KCB KBE

President, Tube Investments; Chairman, Equity Capital for Industry

Dr William Plowden

Director-General, Royal Institute of Public Administration

| | |
|---|---|
| Sir Joseph Pope | Chairman, TecQuipment, Nottingham |
| James F. Porter | Director, Commonwealth Institute |
| Cedric Price | Architect |
| Christopher Price | Pro-Assistant Director, Polytechnic of the South Bank |
| Air Marshal Sir Charles Pringle KBE | Director and Chief Executive, The Society of British Aerospace Companies |
| A.J.R. Purssell | formerly Joint Deputy Chairman, Arthur Guinness and Sons |
| A.S. Railton | Director, Anduff Car Wash |
| Tim Rathbone MP | Member of Parliament for Lewes (Conservative) |
| J.W. Ray | Managing Director, Catnic Components |
| Sir John Read | Chairman: Central Board, Trustee Savings Bank, United Dominions Trust; Deputy Chairman, Thames Television |
| Professor H.A. Rée | formerly Professor of Education, University of York |
| The Lord Reilly | Chairman, Race International Designs; formerly Director, Design Council |
| Professor R.W. Revans | Founder, Action Learning Trust |

| | |
|---|---|
| K.J. Revell | formerly Director of Education, Croydon |
| James T. Reynolds | formerly Chairman, British Thornton |
| Sir Peter Reynolds CBE | Chairman, Rank Hovis |
| Clive Richards | Director, Clive Richards & Co. |
| Dr Raymond Rickett CBE | Director, Middlesex Polytechnic |
| T.J. Rix | Chief Executive, Longman Group |
| Dr R.F.M. Robbins | Director, Plymouth Polytechnic |
| The Rt Hon Sir Kenneth Robinson | Treasurer, Royal Society of Arts; formerly Chairman, Arts Council |
| T. Lloyd Robinson TD | Vice-Chairman, Legal and General Assurance Society |
| Richard Rogers | Richard Rogers & Partners (Architects) |
| Sir Denis Rooke CBE FRS | Chairman, British Gas Corporation |
| Dr W. Bonney Rust OBE | formerly Principal, Hammersmith and West London College |
| The Hon Timothy Sainsbury MP | Member of Parliament for Hove (Conservative); Director, J Sainsbury |
| Sir Francis Sandilands CBE | formerly Chairman, Commercial Union Assurance |

| | |
|---|---|
| The Rt Hon Lady Seear | Liberal leader in the House of Lords |
| The Lord Seebohm TD | formerly Chairman: Finance for Industry, Joseph Rowntree Memorial Trust |
| The Rt Hon Earl of Selkirk KT GCMG GBE SFC QC | formerly First Lord of the Admiralty, UK Commissioner for Singapore |
| The Rt Rev David Sheppard | Bishop of Liverpool |
| The Hon David Sieff | Director, Marks and Spencer |
| Sir George Sinclair CMG OBE | Chairman, Association of Governing Bodies of Independent Schools |
| Sir Alex Smith | formerly Director, Manchester Polytechnic |
| Brian Smith | Consultant; formerly Professor of Design Management, Royal College of Art |
| The Earl of Snowdon GCVO RDI | Photographer; Artistic Adviser to *The Sunday Times* |
| Sir Sigmund Sternberg JP | Chairman, Commodities Research Unit; Lloyds Underwriter |
| Sir Roy Strong | Director, Victoria and Albert Museum |
| Sir Arthur Sugden | Director, Manchester Ship Canal |

| | |
|---|---|
| Charles Swallow | Director, Vanderbilt Racquet Club; formerly Head, Mount Grace School, Potters Bar, Herts |
| The Lord Swann FRS | formerly Vice-Chancellor, University of Edinburgh; Chairman, BBC; Chairman, Technical Change Centre |
| John Swire | Chairman, John Swire & Sons; Hon President, Cathay Pacific Airways |
| Saxon Tate | Chief Executive, Industrial Development Board for Northern Ireland |
| The Lord Taylor of Hadfield | Founder and Life President, Taylor Woodrow Group |
| The Rt Hon Lord Thomson of Monifieth KT | Chairman, Independent Broadcasting Authority; formerly Commissioner, EEC |
| Professor Bryan Thwaites | Co-Chairman, Education 2000, Southampton University; formerly Principal, Westfield College |
| Charles H Tidbury | Chairman, Whitbread & Co. |
| The Lord Todd OM FRS | formerly Master, Christ's College, Cambridge |
| Rev Canon George Tolley | Head, Quality Branch, Manpower Services Commission |
| Sir Francis Tombs | Director, N.M. Rothschild & Son; Chairman, The Engineering Council |

Professor John Tomlinson CBE Professor of Education and Director of the Institute of Education of Warwick University

Donald Trelford · Editor, the *Observer*

Professor Sir Peter Trench CBE Chairman, National House Building Council

Anthony C Verity · Headmaster, Leeds Grammar School

Sir Ralph Verney · formerly Chairman, Nature
Bt KBE DL JP · Conservancy Council

W.M. Vernon · Chairman, Famous Names; Director, Strong & Fisher (Holdings)

Sir Charles Villiers MC · Chairman, BSC (Industry)

Sir Peter Walters · Chairman, BP

Sir Toby Weaver CB · Formerly Deputy Secretary, Department of Education and Science

Dr John Wedgwood · Medical Director, Royal Hospital and Home for for Incurables, Putney, London

W.L. Weinstein · Fellow and Tutor in Politics, Balliol College, Oxford

The Lord Weinstock · Managing Director, General Electric

Professor J.C. West CBE · Vice-Chancellor and Principal, University of Bradford

Phillip Whitehead

Executive Producer, Brook Productions

Professor Ray Wild

Head, Department of Engineering and Management Systems, Brunel University

Jean R.F. Wilks CBE

formerly Headmistress, King Edward VI High School for Girls, Birmingham; President, Association of Head Mistresses

G. Winfield

Chief Executive, Overseas Division, BOC Group

The Rt Hon Lord Young of Graffham

formerly Minister without Portfolio

# Appendix 2

**Members of the Education for Capability Committee**


**Professor John Ashworth**                     1981–
Vice-Chancellor, University of Salford

**Mr Gordon Bell**                              1985–
Headmaster, Norton Priory School,
Runcorn

**Mr Tom Blumenau**                             1980–
Managing Director, Rexgrove Ltd., London

**Professor Daphne Brooker**                    1979–84
Head of Fashion, Kingston Polytechnic

**The Rt Hon Lord Brown MBE**                   1979–80
formerly Chairman, Glacier Metal Co.

**Mr Tyrrell Burgess**                          1979–
Reader in the Philosophy of Social
Institutions and Dean of Continuing
Education, North East London Polytechnic

**Professor John Cowan**                        1985–
Department of Civil Engineering,
Heriot-Watt University, Edinburgh

**Mr Michael Forman**                           1982–
Group Personnel Director, TI Group

**Mr Peter Gorb**                               1979–
Senior Fellow in Design Management,        (Chairman, 1979–83)
London Business School

**Mr Robin Guthrie**                                    1984–
Director, Joseph Rowntree Memorial Trust

**Professor Charles Handy**                             1979–
Visiting Professor, London Business School(Chairman, 1983–)

**Dame Diana Reader Harris DBE**                        1979–82
formerly Headmistress, Sherborne School
for Girls; Vice-President, Royal Society
of Arts

**Professor Peter Herriot**                            1979–80
Head, Department of Occupational
Psychology, Birkbeck College, University
of London

**Sir Ian Hunter MBE**                                 1979–83
Chairman and Managing Director,
Harold Holt; Vice-President,
Royal Society of Arts

**Mr Alan Hutchinson JP**                              1982–
Principal, Paddington College

**Mrs Anne Jones**                                     1983–
Head, Cranford Community School,
Hounslow, Middlesex

**Professor Douglas Lewin**                            1981–84
Professor of Electronics,
University of East Anglia

**Mr Richard Martineau**                               1985–
Specialist Director of Social Policy,
Whitbread and Company

**Mr Geoffrey Melling**                                1985–
Director, The Further Education Staff
College

**Dame Margaret Miles DBE**     1980–85
formerly Headmistress, Mayfield School,
London

**Mr Martin Moss CBE**     1983–85
Director, National Trust (Enterprises);
Vice-President, Royal Society of Arts

**Dr Patrick Nuttgens CBE**     1979–
Director, Leeds Polytechnic

**Sir Alex Smith**     1981–84
formerly Director, Manchester Polytechnic

**Mr Charles Swallow**     1982–
Director, Vanderbilt Racquet Club;
formerly Head, Mount Grace School,
Potters Bar, Herts

**The Rev Canon George Tolley**     1983–
Manpower Services Commission

**Professor John Tomlinson CBE**     1981–
Professor of Education and Director of
the Institute of Education at
Warwick University

**Sir Toby Weaver CB**     1979–
formerly Deputy Secretary, Department
of Education and Science